MW01242464

She doesn't tiptoe around the "hard-stuff."

Fun and "games."

What **every girl** should know. Something for every age—
From 6 to 96.

True! True! True!

Even the recipes are good but not enough of them.

She's **been there** and done that (or you have!)

Wisdom, wit, whimsy and winsome.

Oh, lady be good!

She must have known **MY** mama.

A book you can pick up and put down-----but not for long!
Every page will get a smile and a nod (or maybe a frown?)

A "spirit lifter," perfect **GIFTer** of a book.

Plain-plain-plain-good! An easy read.

With so much infinite variety, it's never boring.

Mama MIA!

I've tried all the recipes, and they are good and easy.

Not a throw away book. You'll probably buy several for
gift-giving, but want to keep your own—after all,
you'll underline half of it.

Every bride should have one of these books (and give one to
each of her bridesmaids). Great fun to read at a bridal shower.

Mama Said...

A Sparkling Treasure Trove of Sage Advice
Full of Warmth and Humor with a Modern Twist
of "How-To" For Women to Work Their Wiles.

Laugh & enjoy!

Martha Hammons

2005

Mama Said...

A Sparkling Treasure Trove of Sage Advice
full of Warmth and Humor with a Modern Twist
of "How-To" for Women to Work Their Wiles.

MARTHA HOUSTON REID HAMMOND

Little snippets of wisdom and guidance . . .
it's personal; it has grace and charm; it's funny and true;
it's common sense and real experiences; it's plain speaking and Southern;
it's probably what you've told your daughters
or remember your "Mama Said . . ."

Often hilarious . . . Always poignant!

Hennypenny Press

Corinth, Mississippi

Copyright © 2003
by Martha Houston Reid Hammond

ISBN 0-9746988-0-6

All Rights Reserved.
No part of this book may be reproduced, stored in a retrieval
system, or transmitted by any means, electronic, mechanical,
photocopying, recording, or otherwise,
without written permission from the author.

Printed in the United States of America
Third printing

Back cover photo by Sue Elam
Design by Cynthia Clark
Sketches by Susan Sellers

Hennypenny Press
c/o Reid Brothers Incorporated • P.O. Box 905 • Corinth, Ms 38834
662-286-2869 • email: cokeman@nadata.net

Please call, write or email: to the above address to purchase our book.

Dedication

This book is dedicated to my three daughters,
Shannon, Courtney, Shelby,
and in loving memory of their sister, Candy.

Too: To my granddaughters
Shelby, Leigh and Courtney Umstattd;
Yancy Love; and Shannon and Annie Flaten

Acknowledgements

Heartfelt thanks to my daughters, **Shannon** and **Courtney**, for their input (leave it in) and their output (take it out), their hard work typing and retyping, and their encouragement and giggles and love; to daughter, **Shelby**, who contributed and inspired and who gives me delight and laughter and a youthful perspective.

To **Barney**, my favorite son, who is helpful in all my endeavors and has requested that I please not write a book of instructions for him; to **Thomas Hal Phillips**, author and friend, who encouraged us from the very beginning; to **Dot Mann** whose enthusiasm and confidence in us meant a great deal; to **"Sam" Thompson**, who helped me avoid pitfalls and gave me some insight to the publishing business. Her friendship is cherished. To **Alisa Pittman** for her friendship and encouragement; to **Susan Sellers** for her help and artistic talent who, under intense pressure, helped us finalize our project. To **Barney McKee**, kind, patient and helpful consultant, publisher of Quail Ridge Press; and to **Cyndi Clark**, his most able and talented graphic artist whose help was immeasurable. Most importantly, my love and thanks to **Doug** who "dug-up" all this stuff from here, there and yon and said, "You've got to do this." Then he started typing . . .

Preface

Sometime in the late '60s, Martha began collecting various ideas, suggestions, tidbits of information and other thoughts she had, especially for her girls. She has devoted her life to directing them as they spread their wings and grew into adulthood. These thoughts reflect her taste, personality, humor, and give them much insight into what life is all about. They were jotted on scraps of paper, church bulletins, napkins, envelopes, spiral notebooks, recipe cards, etc. We called them *Mama Said* . . . We felt the compelling need to share these thoughts as much as possible, and they are presented here in the same disarray as they were saved.

It has been a joy and privilege (and still is) to have been a part of this lady's life and to have shared the happy times, the heartaches, hopes, fears and dreams of our family.

Doug

AND THE BEAT GOES ON . . .
Well, dear ones, Mama is still talking with many new up-dated opinions and advice. The pages in this book reveal more of her wit and wisdom(?), ideas and experiences to hopefully help smooth out the bumps in the life of her darling daughters(3) granddaughters (6) and yours.

A Letter to My Girls

Dear Ones,

I admit that this book is not spellbinding, or tightly plotted and compactly written. It is not riveting or powerful or thrilling. I would like to think that it is at least a bit enthralling, interesting, and perhaps delightful enough to keep you reading until the end—make you laugh, agree, wonder, contemplate, "roll-your-eyes," shake your head (yea or nay) and understand that the ideas are written at random and in complete disarray—a hodgepodge of thoughts collected especially for you from me with a twinkle in my eyes and love in my heart—and "tongue in cheek."

Mama

If you want to keep a **friend**, do nice things for her children. If you want to lose a friend, try to hire her housekeeper. Both gestures will always be remembered (with opposite reactions, of course).

 Use a long handled spoon when cooking **grits**, because they often pop out and burn your hand.

> If your husband is the type who walks away while you are talking to him (especially if it is an **argument**), the only solution I have found is wait until you are driving in the car to tackle a subject you want him to listen to. Either you will have his attention, or he will have to jump out of the car.

The best time to ask your husband for a **favor** or advice is in the morning, preferably after breakfast, but before he's in a hurry to go to work. After supper is OK if he's had a good day, but not if he comes home tired and irritable. After he's enjoyed a good meal, put it to him.

Do not believe plumbers, paper hangers, electricians, carpenters and painters. Of course there are exceptions, but most of them do not show up when they **promise**. It is wise not to pay until the job is finished. They will ask for part payment when the work is partially done, and they will never show up again or wait weeks or months to finish the job you expected to be finished in a few days.

They say chocolate relieves stress. I believe it. (But if it doesn't, so what!?!)

 On matters of **inheritance**: When a relative dies and inheritance is involved, people who have loved each other forever and never had a cross word, can turn into scheming, conniving, selfish strangers.

When you look up a **telephone** number, say it out loud. That way, you not only see it and think it—you hear it also. That's three impressions, and it really helps. How many times have you looked up a number, closed the book and then forgotten what it was?

Choose **paint** colors for your rooms in your house that are most becoming to you.

♪ If you are late for **church**, try to go in while the congregation is standing to sing, etc. Then it will not be as noticeable as when all are seated, and you are standing. The same is true if you must leave the service early.

> I have rarely been sorry that I have kept my **mouth shut.** I have often been sorry that I have opened it.

Fresh **flowers** (even just one) in the guest room make your guest feel welcome and important.

When giving a party honoring a **bride**, a graduate, etc., try to give the first party—they appreciate it more and enjoy it more (than the fifth party, etc.). The same is true when giving a gift to a bride, graduate, etc.

If a child has an **earache**, do not fool around. Take him/her to a doctor at once. Give medicines that the doctor prescribes until it is all gone (not till there is no complaint about the ear). Ear pain is terrible! If throat is red, be sure to tend to it before infection spreads to the ears and vice-versa.

A woman who wears lots of **diamonds** does so for one of three reasons:
1. She wants to show off "her" money.
2. Her husband wants her to show off "his" money.
3. She and her family have always had lots of money, and she was "raised" wearing real jewelry and thinks nothing of it.

Usually you can tell by looking at her other clothes and hair style and listening to her talk, which of the three reasons fits her.

Lord, keep your arm around my shoulders and your hand over my mouth. (So I won't put my foot in it).

The most welcome **guests** are those who know when to leave.

Sometimes men may try to **be more attractive** by laughing louder, telling dirty jokes, using more curse words, giving presents, spending more money, flirting outrageously, drinking heavily. If they could only realize that it makes them more unattractive to most of us. (Also, during this frustrating period of their lives, they get jealous very easily, usually over nothing, and often mostly imagined.)

Try to sit with your **child** during his/her meal, even if you are not eating. This is a good idea with your husband, too.

> Some men are **struck blind** when they open the refrigerator door. They just stand there and expect whatever they're looking for to jump into their hands. If you have moved the milk, mayo, jelly, butter, etc. from its usual place, they cannot see it even if it is right in front of them, perhaps on another shelf or moved to the right or left. Some of my friends say the same about their husbands and sons—never about daughters. It must be a male thing.

To a man his **genital** area is a marvelous wonder to behold. He is proud of his penis and testicles and is quite interested in them from early childhood until he dies. All of his sexual prowess, manliness, and his "special ideas of himself" are centered there. He can see them and touch them everyday—often. Men expect their women to feel the same way as they do about this most special, sensitive place between their legs. This has been proven for eons. Some women do; some don't, some pretend.

Be sure to flush all **toilets** when leaving home for a few days. Also, make certain the fridge and freezer doors are closed.

Mama doin' the
Bug Boogie

Nightgown Gardening
Summertime

I have found that the most pleasant kind of gardening is in my nightgown. Nightgown gardening can only be done in the early morning. It is the very best time for picking off dead blooms, cutting a few blossoms for the house, inspecting plants, turning a few pots around for different light, and watering those on the deck or patio.

No one can see me. I feel "loose" and cool. Water always runs down my arms as I reach to water the hanging plants. I do not like it but am not tall enough to prevent it. Well, I could stand on something, but its too much trouble, so part of me and my gown are always wet by the time I go inside. Also leaves and sometimes dirt are stuck to my gown, but still puttering around in my nightgown early in the morning is utterly delightful. Sometimes I venture out front to get the paper because no neighbors or cars are up and out—but yesterday our neighbor caught me as he went (fully dressed) to get his morning paper. "Morning Martha" he said as he reached in his box, turned and went back toward his house with his head down scanning the news. I could have been in a Halloween costume wearing a mask, for all the attention he paid. He might have noticed if I had been naked, but I am not sure. Anyway—I was in my cool, comfortable nightgown and loving the morning.

P.S. Sometimes a bug gets on my back or crawls up my leg. Then I do the "bug-boogie." It's not very graceful but very energetic and brief (until the bug is off).

If you have looked everywhere for an article of clothing and cannot find it, look in the **dryer**.

Do not ever **write** something down you would mind someone reading (other than the recipient of your note). If it's to a boyfriend, his mother or roommate or someone else will see it sooner or later. If to a friend or relative, relationships may change. Never write down something you may be ashamed of or have to "take back." Be very careful what is written by your hand and signed with your name.

When calling **older people** or friends with small children on the phone, let it ring more times than usual. It takes older folks longer to get to the phone, and mothers may be busy with babies and cannot "let go" at that very second.

If you think you are wearing too much **jewelry**, you are wearing too much jewelry.

After seeing a **bumper sticker** saying, "God is my co-pilot," our preacher entitled a sermon "If God is your co-pilot, you are in the wrong seat." That says it all . . . but of course, that is not all he said.

If expecting **"to make love"** either day or night, take the telephone off the hook for a while. When it rings, the mood is broken, even if you don't answer it.

A good **friend** will laugh with you and cry with you and always try to help when needed. She will also share the flowers from her yard.

When visiting in a **foreign country**, do not complain if everything is not as it is in the United States. It is not supposed to be the same. Accept each difference as interesting. Do not complain because of inconvenience. Perhaps there is no hot water, or perhaps their hot water is warm and their cold drinks are cool. Be careful of drinking water but do not announce your consternation in a loud voice. Behave as if you were a guest in the home of a friend—accepting the plans, the hospitality, habits, as you would those of a gracious host. "When in Rome, do as the Romans do." (Not new, but still true.)

❀ ❀ ❀

Every spring I wish I had planted more **bulbs** in the fall!

Don't overestimate yourself by **marrying a man** thinking you will change him. If he is "cheap," has a habit of being late all the time, lies even a little, drinks a lot, etc., nothing you do after marriage will change him. In fact, as years go by, the bad habits will magnify and get worse and worse no matter what methods you employ. If you don't like him just the way he is, then back out before it is too late. He will not change, except perhaps, temporarily.

It is more fun to have wrinkles caused by laughter than by frowns.

Doctor George W. Crane wrote a very popular newspaper column years ago called "The Worry Clinic." He advocated women feign ardor whether they were "in the mood" or not. Many women do not realize the different erotic hungers of husband and wife, the husband's being much stronger and more often. Dr. Crane recommended **"boudoir cheesecake,"** a recipe that's worked for thousands of years. Wives, nothing washes out a husband's irritation and grouchy criticisms like an emotional dose of boudoir cheesecake. It's a recipe for a happy man. (Could this be why Victoria's Secret is so successful?).

When attending a piano (or any music **recital** or opera), never be the first to applaud as it may not be the end of the piece, even though there is a long pause, and it seems to have ended.

Do not leave your **laundry or sleepwear** on the floor, chair or door knob. If it has any sex appeal while you are wearing it, it is all lost when constantly seen in such an untidy manner. However, do not  expect the same of your husband as he will probably leave his dirty underwear and socks exactly where he took them off (for you to pick up)—unromantic, but true.

Stop at every **lemonade stand** that you can and buy from those excited, happy children. It doesn't matter if you know them or not, but be sure to stop at the ones in your neighborhood. (Their parents will appreciate it more than the children.) If you can't drink it, take it with you and pour it out—out of sight!

When renting or buying a house, be sure the **commodes** flush well. Throw a spoonful of dry coffee grounds in and then flush. If they go down, fine. If some are left and float on top, something is wrong. Not enough water pressure or something. This can be a most unwelcome problem.

Use a dark **wash cloth** (rust, brown, navy, wine, etc.) to wash your face. You may ruin a light colored one with makeup, etc. Pack your own for travel to a friend's house (so you won't stain theirs) or use the new "wipe-cleansers" available now that you can throw away.

Some people bring **joy** wherever they go. Some, whenever they go. Try to be the former whenever and wherever you can.

If you have a good **yard man**, do not "announce it to the world," unless you want to share his time with all your friends. This stands for baby sitters, too. It sounds silly but is really self-preservation. Pay both well. (Yes, I admit this is not nice or neighborly.)

❀ ✿ ❀

When installing a **showerhead**, be
sure not to install it too high for you.
Plumbers always set it at the correct
height for men, and consequently the
water hits you on the head or in the
face. Have it lowered so that you may take a shower without the water hitting you in the face or in your hair (by standing back a bit). Also, see that the soap dish is out of the way of the shower spray. Tons of soap is washed away because the soap dishes are hit by the spray when the shower is on.

A GRAY FEBRUARY DAY

"This is the day the Lord hath made.
Let us rejoice and be glad in it." Psalm 118:24

Though it's cold and wet outside. I awoke this morning in a warm, comfortable home. **"REJOICE."** I was hungry for breakfast (and lunch and supper) a blessing, as many do not hunger due to illness or worry, and there was plenty of food. **"REJOICE."** I had work to do and was able to do it. **"REJOICE."** I communicated in person and by telephone with my loving family and friends. **"REJOICE."** I am not in pain. **"REJOICE."** I had the pleasure of doing something good for someone. "I am glad." My burdens, though they change from time to time, are real but I know that God will not give me more than I can carry and he will help me. **"REJOICE."** I can see and hear the signs of approaching springtime, and I am glad. **"REJOICE."**

This evening I will find rest and a peaceful night in the comfort of my warm bed. **"REJOICE"** and **AMEN.**

When in church, sing all the hymns.
Then when you are 40 and cannot see the
words, you can at least sing the first verse.

27

There is no getting around the fact that **teenagers** at some point take a vow of silence. You can, however, learn the meaning of some of their responses—looking at the ceiling with their eyes rolled back in their head (please not that again); mouth half opened, nose wrinkled up, eyes squinty (what !); eyes shut, head to one side (I hear you).   Just realize that sooner or later, they will look at you with an appealing smile and say, "I need a little money" or "How about the keys to the car?"

❀ ✿ ❀

If you **think** you can't or you think you can, you are right. Mama said, "can't never could."

❀ ✿ ❀

Here in the South, **when a friend or relative dies**, many casseroles, cakes, pies, hams, and salads are brought to the house of the deceased in order to feed all who have come there after the funeral or are staying there.

There is an immediate need for paper products—plates, (2 sizes), napkins, foil, plastic wrap, plastic bowls, paper towels, garbage bags, cups (2 sizes) sodas and coffee. If you can leave a box of all or some of the supplies at the house of the deceased early on the first day, they will be very handy and appreciated. A cooler of ice may also be useful. Later if you wish, you may send a memorial. (If you do some of the above, it is not necessary to send flowers, too.)

Never fail easy recipe

Apple Salad
(Very refreshing)

- 2 or 3 crisp apples (Fiji, etc.) peeled or not—
  I like peeled, but it is not as pretty. Chopped
  (not small)
- $\frac{1}{2}$ (more or less) 8 oz. carton Cool Whip (reg. or
  lite)
- 1 ($8\frac{1}{2}$ oz.) can crushed pineapple in syrup
  drained, (can use it in its own juice, but it is
  not as sweet) or larger ($15\frac{1}{2}$ oz.) can if you
  use 4 or 5 apples which will make a lot.

Stir all together—enjoy!! (Can add chopped
pecans or small marshmallows, or both).

 **Ahhh romance**—Flowers and candy, secret glances and meetings, parties and dancing—all that goes with falling in love is wonderful and romantic; but later when you are married, candy makes you fat; flowers don't last and you would rather have a new pair of shoes. You prefer your husband to take out the trash instead of taking you out dancing. Circumstances change, but still romance flourishes in other ways—his arm across the back of the church pew, and a squeeze on your shoulder, a kiss goodbye in the morning, a hug when he gets home, keeping your car filled with gas, commenting on how nice you look (all this works both ways), <u>slow dancing in the kitchen when there is no music,</u> a secret smile and a gleam in his eye, across a room full of people. Keep romance alive! You can do it!!!

Bittersweet **chocolate** has more intense taste than semisweet, but they can be used interchangeably.

Only have all-purpose flour on hand, but need **self rising**? Just mix 1½ teaspoons of baking powder with ½ teaspoon salt into 1 cup all-purpose flour, and you did it yourself!

If you have pet **birds**, don't allow any seeds to get into the sink. Often they will sprout down in the drain and eventually cause a mat that causes the drain to stop up. Best to clean cage, replenish seed, and change the paper in bottom of cage—all on a spread out newspaper. Then fold up newspaper and throw in garbage.

> I love and adore a **polite** driver; I hate and abhor a rude one.

Keep a **list** (for years) of all the entertaining you do, supper, parties, etc., and for brides. List the people invited, what you served, where you had it, who if any, were the co hostesses and the date. I keep my list in a spiral notebook (some are stuck in my favorite cookbook). This helps you not to serve the same thing to people you invite often. Also, reminds you whom you have had.

If you plan to **entertain** anyway, try to have the event when you or a friend have a guest, and say it is to honor him or her (or on a friend's birthday, etc.)

Don't **smoke**! It makes your teeth yellow and your breath smell bad, (nobody will want to kiss you), and your clothes smell terrible, AND it's hazardous to your health!!!!

Only nerds and Don Juans play the **kiss** and tell game. The guys with the hottest stories to tell about their romantic escapades, don't. They are called gentlemen. They can be firemen, policemen, farmers, garbage collectors, storekeepers, teachers or Mr. Richie Rich—blessed be the gentleman!

❀ ✿ ❀

A good time to have a **party** is:
1. Before a dance (game, concert). People come and go before it gets too late (cocktail supper, etc.)
2. When your yard is pretty—or when you have plenty of flowers to cut and put into the house.
3. Right after you bring your plants (that have been on the deck, patio, etc.) in to protect them from the weather. Do it before they get the winter "droops." Your house will look pretty with all the fresh greenery.
4. Usually February and March are good times to entertain as there is not very much going on. The first Christmas party, Thanksgiving party, or summer party is fine, but later people are entertained so much during holidays that they would just as soon stay home, so do not entertain when everyone else is.

❀ ✿ ❀

When purchasing containers for **leftovers** in refrigerator, buy clear ones. Often you must lift the tops off colored ones to see what's inside.

Be proud of your Southern **heritage** and don't apologize for your Southern accent—it's charming, usually, but be sure your grammar is correct. Our choice of words may be different from what Yankees would choose, but we mean the same thing. We say, "I'm fixin' supper." They say, "I'm making dinner." What's the big deal?????

You don't find **life** worth living. You make it that way.

"Stink," "squat," and "armpit" are not **words** ladies should use. They are just unpleasant sounding. Add "crap" to that list, too. (Once a plumber asked me to "hunker-down" and look at a pipe leak—much better than "squat.")

I met him, I liked him.
I liked him, I loved him.
I loved him, I let him.
I let him, I **lost** him.

Ladies should move silently and with grace. We hear more interesting tidbits that way; also, a subtle roll of your hips is very **ladylike** and graceful. I mean, what man would do that???

When calling about plane **tickets**, arrival times, etc., be sure and ask "What Gate?" This will save much time and walking.

It is much easier and more fun to "take" children to **camp** than to pick them up afterwards. On the way, everything is well packed, and the children are happy and excited. Coming home everything is dirty, wet, and sandy and the overall mood is not as good as the trip to camp. If possible, take <u>and</u> pick up! (Your child will be so glad to see you.)

When glancing thru the paper or a magazine (there is never time to **READ** a magazine with children in the house), usually a child will appear within a very few minutes, either mad, with a skinned knee or asking you to do something. They will appear even sooner if you place a cup of hot tea, an iced beverage, or coffee by your side. An appearance by your side always involves something that will make you leave your spot until the hot beverage is cold or the ice has melted. Here are two sure fire techniques for finding your children—however, they also work when you do not want them to . . . unfortunately. Get on the telephone or go to the bathroom, and here one comes.

When at the **circus**, be sure and sit on the side opposite the band. Most of the acts face that side and have their backs to the band. This way you face the band and the acts face you. Also, the band will not appear as loud. Many little children dislike the loudness of parades and loud music close by.

Don't blame your children's friends for the shortcomings of their **parents**—such as in not reciprocating a visit, a meal, or spending the night.

Tuesdays or Thursday nights are good times for a dinner **party**, etc. It doesn't crowd the weekend activities and most people will go home early because they have to work the next day. They can always make their own weekend plans for later. Also, if you need to hire extra help, they are easier to find in middle of the week. Too, some charge more on weekends.

Often a sweater or blouse (sometimes a dress) can be worn **backwards**. A shell or tank almost always. If you spill something on the front, just go to the nearest private place and turn it around. Of course, this works best if you are wearing a jacket or cardigan on top.

In **church**, you always see several people who do not sing. . . . Often it's because they do not have their glasses and cannot see.

> If your **builder** says your home will be ready in November, don't expect it until February. If he is building a patio, carport, any addition, and says it will be ready in May, it won't. Perhaps by the end of June. No matter what they promise, it always takes longer, for sure. (and always costs more).

It is not a good policy to lend **money** or property of great worth to a friend or relative. They often feel that your close relationship means they do not have to pay it back, and your relationship will soon come to an end. The same holds true about employees. There is no way to have an employer/employee relationship with friends or relatives. Always friction and resentfulness will show up.

When you and your husband or companion are **flying** somewhere and need a ticket, or get seat assignments, etc., get in two different lines. Whoever gets to the counter first can handle both of your tickets, and the other can drop out of their line. It usually shortens waiting time.

Wherever you live, find a good plumber, painter, or carpenter and electrician. When you use him, pay him promptly. If you find an honest one who does good work, you are extremely **lucky**; if he is dependable, you are very rich.

❀ ✿ ❀

Look after **each other**, back each other up, help each other, encourage each other, love each other, and never lose touch with each other. Make an effort to get together. Never lose your faith.

❀ ✿ ❀

❀ ✿ ❀

A written **"thank-you"** is not always necessary, but it is always appropriate and always appreciated. It is doing that little bit extra by taking time to write, that really shows appreciation. So many people never write a "thank you." Don't be one of them. (A phone call or e-mail is better than nothing.)

If you will keep a small book or pamphlet in the pocket of your car, you will find that **waiting** for the children to get out of school or the dentist, or whatever, will not be such an impatient wait. *The Upper Room, Readers Digest,* plus *The Magazine of Positive Thinking* (Dr. Peale's brief sermons), etc. are very good ones.

It is easier to **forgive** than to forget, but if you cannot forget, have you really forgiven?

Don't tell everything you know.

Easy **gardening** tips: To make a bigger visual impact use several large pots planted lavishly with blooming plants and trailing vines rather than numerous small pots. Use a slow-release fertilizer on everything. Using a water soluble fertilizer helps keep container blooming plants pretty all summer.

Loosen tops of **jars** before refrigeration, so that they will not be so difficult to open when you take them out of the fridge. Cold expands, heat shrinks.

Keep a "running list" all thru the year of the wedding **invitations** you have received and the gifts you have sent. It will come in mighty handy when it is your turn to send invitations.

> The best way to avoid a household **pest**—is don't let him retire.

If you have a **concrete** floor in carport or parking area, have it understood by the builder in the beginning, that you do not want it to hold puddles of water after a hard rain. Make sure it drains away from the house.

Sleep is a necessary body-balm. Studies show that any degree of sleep depravation will impair performance, both physically and mentally. Sleep is imperative for your body and brain to rest, recuperate, and heal. For years, doctors have said, "Get plenty of bed-rest." That does not mean watching TV, lounging around, or sitting on pillows study- ing, paying bills, etc. REST is a good four-letter word. (Yes, it can be overdone. Exercise is important, too.)

If there is a damaging **storm,** especially hail—be sure to check your car and roofs. Your insurance should cover any damages, dents, tears, etc. Also, if you lose a silver spoon (fork, etc.) or something valuable in your home is lost or damaged, be sure to report to insurance company immediately for proper collection or replacement.

> If you have too much to do or feel **overburdened** with things that must be done, get up earlier for a day or two. Several early morning hours allow you to accomplish almost as much as several extra days. You won't be distracted, and you'll be fresh and feel more like getting things done. Also, your attitude will be improved.

One of the happiest days of the year is right after **Christmas**. The tree is out of the house, and all the decorations are put away . . . no wreath on the door or bow on the lamppost. Be sure all is done before New Year's Day.

If your **mother-in-law** (or father-in-law) asks you what pieces of furniture you wish to inherit, always say, "We would like this or we would like that"—not "I"—as, of course, they are most interested in their son's wishes—not what you want. Tactfully, ask that they tape his name to the piece in the back where it is not easily seen.

If you know the family well, the best time to take food to a house after a **death** is a week or so later, as they usually have plenty the day of the funeral. Try to take it in a container that does not have to be returned, or tape your name on the container if it does have to come back to you.

Your husband may have a **disease**, vasectomy or operation (hernia, prostate, etc.) which may leave him impotent (usually temporarily), not for a physical reason but mentally and emotionally. Being powerless and not being able to perform (as he had previously done) can cause severe depression and change a man's whole image of himself, his personality, and his association with others. This is especially true if it happens in the 40-60 age time frame.

Remember, when you marry a man you also marry his family — for better or worse.

Usually the right angle to approach a difficult **problem** is a "try-angle."

Keep your **closet** doors shut. The room looks better, less cluttered . . . and I think you sleep better.

After **bathing** or swimming, take the towel and push back the cuticles of your fingernails. A good time to give yourself a pedicure is after a bath or shower when skin around the nails is soft.

> The friends you keep determine the **troubles** you meet.

Grandchildren are the rewards I get for not strangling you when you were teenagers. Thank you! Thank you! Thank you!

If you are going to freeze a **casserole**, it does better in a large flat dish than a smaller deep one. It will heat more evenly and quicker. In a deep dish, the top and outside get very hot while it is still cold in the middle. Of course, if the casserole is not to be frozen, put it in any dish available.

If possible on an **airplane**, sit towards the back. In most pictures, after some problem, only the tail section remains intact so perhaps this is the safest place.

It's nice to have a **bank account** of your own, however small, so that you can occasionally buy something you want or need without having to explain why you spent so much on face cream or a fabulous pair of pants or a new lamp or rug.

If a **relative** or **friend** indicates that he/she wants to give you something (furniture, silver, china, jewelry, etc.), take it now with much appreciation. After death, you may not get it as there is only "your" word that it was to be yours. Do not feel as if you are stripping their home. They would not offer it if they did not want you to have it. Let them have the pleasure of giving it to you while they are alive, so they can see you enjoy it and know of your appreciation. More hard feelings develop between relatives when they are dividing property.

Most towel racks in ladies' **restrooms** are too high. When you reach for a towel, the water runs down your arm.

If a friend of yours is having a lot of **company** for a few days, offer to make a salad, desert or casserole to help out in the food department, or take something over before the guests arrive.

Sometimes I don't want to get ready to go to **church**, and I would rather do something else, or I think of a "good reason" not to go. Then, usually I go anyway, and I am always glad I did. Our souls need to be fed just as regularly as our bodies need food to survive. Church, prayer, etc., only on holidays or when we feel dire need, does not support our soul anymore than one meal a week can support our bodies.

> **Never have so much pride that you cannot accept a gift, favor, or compliment with much appreciation and thankfulness from you.**

You need more than one spatula in the **kitchen** . . .
at least two different sizes. It took me years to realize I could buy another pan just like my favorite one that I used most often. Now, one is always handy when the other is on the stove or in the dishwasher.

My favorite religious holiday is **Easter** with its uplifting sense of hope and renewal. Where I live, Easter also brings blooming dogwood trees, azaleas, Lily of the Valley and violets. For some reason though, many Easters are so cold the little girls wearing their pretty dresses must add a sweater or coat. Remember this—without Easter, we would have no reason to celebrate Christmas.

A light-colored **counter** in the kitchen and bath are better than dark ones for many reasons—they do not show dust, powder, stains, etc., as easily; reflect more light, etc. Dark floors show crumbs.

If your **children** are close by but do not respond when you call them, go into the bathroom. Stand in there a minute, and brush your teeth. If one doesn't appear in a few seconds, get in the shower, tub, or sit on commode. One or two will surely appear or call you as if by magic. Sometimes this same method will work if you are expecting an important phone call. Another method of making your child appear is to sit down, prop your feet up, and start a good book. You'll never finish the first chapter.

Be sure and save all your **luggage** receipts from airplane trips, as this is the only proof you have that you checked the items. It is a good idea to save most receipts anyway. You never can tell when you may need them for proof of purchase, when returning an item, or if an appliance breaks down, to show a warranty is still in effect.

On **rainy days** wear something bright yellow, orange, red, hot pink, etc. It will brighten a gray day—and you, too!

When you would like to do something for a friend of yours who is having a second (or third, etc.) child, be aware that some mothers-to-be are uncomfortable asking their friends to "another" baby shower. A good idea is a **casserole shower**. Tell guests to bring a casserole in a disposable container, labeled with cooking instructions, that can be frozen until needed. Another good idea, very much appreciated, is a **diaper shower**. They never get too many (give different sizes).

When wiping off a table, push chairs under first. Then when you wipe the table, any crumbs you do not pick up will fall on floor rather than in chair seats . . . now sweep, vacuum or let the **dog lick** them up.

When buying a half of a **ham**, always purchase the butt end. It is worth the extra money per pound. Use the first nice slices for meals or sandwiches. When the slices get more fatty, fry them, as most of the fat cooks out. Use the rest, bone, etc. for greens, beans, and peas as seasoning when boiling.

Never allow household **mail** including your personal mail, to be sent to your husband's office or place of work. If you do, you will eventually discover that some of it will be lost, will finally get to you very late, or never.

Do not worry about who does not come to your **funeral**,
for I assure you it does not matter who does not appear.
Of course, we do appreciate those who do make the effort
to come; but if any one really wants to show their love,
affection and friendship, they can best do it by helping or
doing something for your children if and when they have the
opportunity.

It is much easier to **"go"** when your children are small (and
you can leave them in the tender loving care of a baby sitter
or relative) than it is when they are between 12 and 18.
Boys are easier to care for than girls after the age of 6. Before
that they are about the same. All "girl-things" (clubs, games,
clothes, entertainment, etc.) seem to take more time than
"boy-things" . . . and more money!

A **telephone** is an instrument for convenience—not
entertainment! However, it is impossible for teen-age girls to
understand this statement or abide by it, and unfortunately
some of them never outgrow it.

Lines from one of my **favorite hymns**:
"In the bulb there is a flower; in the seed an apple tree; . . .
in our death, a resurrection: at the last, a victory."

(Hymn of Promise by Sleeth)

One of my "famous-quick-easy" recipes

Bride's Delight
(muffins/rolls)

Preheat oven to 400 degrees. Lightly grease muffin pan.

Mix together:
- 2 cups Bisquick
- 1 stick soft (not melted) real butter
- 8 ounces sour cream

Do not beat. Just stir gently 'til it is moistened.

Fill small muffin tins ½ full (makes 24). Bake until golden brown. For large muffins, bake at 375 degrees until golden brown. I like the smaller ones best. Shelby prefers the larger ones. Sometimes the larger ones may take a wee bit longer to be done in the middle. (You do not even need to serve butter.)

P.S. This is an all time favorite recipe because it is so easy and so good! Often I include it with a gift to a bride, and often she thanks me more profusely for the recipe than for the gift.

Do not give any used or **"handed down"** clothing to a "first child" of a friend even though they are in perfect condition. People rarely want or will use "handed down" clothes for their first precious darling. Later, however, when others have arrived, they are very much appreciated.

Before wearing a **swimsuit** or short shorts, be sure to shave your legs smoothly as far up as possible. Nothing is more unsightly than hair showing at the edge of your pants. Also, keep underarms neat.

Fresh flowers do a lot for a room. They make it seem cleaner, more inviting, charming. Next best is green plants— keep green leaves clean. Do not use artificial flowers unless absolutely necessary. In fact, just about anything is better. Dried flowers are nice but do not leave them there forever. Recently, I saw some lovely, bright silk flowers. They would be pretty (for awhile) in winter, when fresh flowers are not available. (Never even consider plastic.)

Do not leave dead or withered flowers in a room. No matter how pretty or clean the room is **withered flowers** seem to attract all the attention and make a room seem dull and uninviting.

Men need the **companionship** of other men. Do not begrudge your boyfriend or husband a night out with the "boys." Do not try to be too inquisitive about where they go or what they do, or what they said—and if you are told any of these particulars, positively do not repeat the information to anyone no matter how trivial it may seem.

Never force a **child** to eat. He will eat if he is hungry. You are not always hungry, are you? Often he will spit-up (not on purpose) if you make him eat, because of fever, stomach upset, or something of which you are not yet aware.

If you place a **flower arrangement** in front of a mirror, it will double your pleasure. Just one rose or a bouquet will look twice as pretty.

Children are happier with their own peers. Do not hesitate (if you have more than one child) to let each have spend the night company, even on the same night. That keeps them occupied and happy. If just one has company, the other will either hang around and bother them or you the whole time. Also, if you must have an extra for meals and a bed, it's no more trouble for two, and you get it over with in one night instead of two.

Go to the **"head man"** to get anything done in a store or office or company. Get to know him or her, whether you have a complaint or request or not. It is always good to know the "one in charge." Results are usually faster and more pleasing.

Never **punish a child** by depriving him of a meal. This is cruelty on your part. Deprive him, instead, of a favorite toy, TV program, etc.

When taking a present to a **new baby**, take a small gift to the older brother or sister too—or just take one to the older child (or children) instead of the new baby. I promise it will be more appreciated by both mother and children. Most "new babies" have more gifts than they can use anyway.

When making **toast**, do not just put a dab of butter in the middle of the bread. Put a little dab on all four corners and most people will eat it all including the crust. They will always eat the middle part whether it has butter on it or not. Toast prepared in the oven is best.

It is best not to wear **white shoes** until after Easter, unless in a warm resort area. (White suede is OK earlier.) Do not wear them after Labor Day.

When someone is **sick**:
1. Visit them at home only if visits are requested.
2. Do not visit in the hospital unless there is a very special reason.
3. Do not ever sit on a sick person's bed. Sometimes just a jiggle is worrisome or painful.
4. Do not talk or laugh loudly, and never stay longer than 10 minutes.
5. Flowers cut from your own garden are best and usually more appreciated. Potted plants from florists are nice.
6. Gifts such as a nice lotion, books, and stationery, are perfect. Stamps, too.

❀ ❀ ❀

You can accomplish almost any-thing in one day if you will start at 5 a.m. (most will be finished prior to noon). Then you can take a nap!

❀ ❀ ❀

Buttermilk and sour cream are OK to use a week or so beyond **expiration date**, also, canned biscuits, rolls, etc. I have used buttermilk 3 weeks past expiration in cornbread and dip, and it was fine.

❀ ❀ ❀

If you find a **bra** you really like, buy at least two. Buy stockings at least two pairs at a time also.

52

I cannot imagine that any man would look forward to **going to bed** with a woman who has her hair rolled up and cream on her face. Use night cream after saying "good night" and, etc., etc., etc.

Try not to have a **radio or TV** in the eating area or bedroom. If you do, conversation will be KILLED, and that is two rooms in which you should be having some form of chit-chat. Often in too many places, communication is squelched because of a ball game or soap opera. If you never put a radio or TV in one of these rooms, they will never be missed. (OK—so some of you disagree.)

Teach your boys and girls to RSVP, accept and regret, at once by phone or card enclosed in the invitation. Also, teach them to write thank-you notes.

> If your husband would rather be in the den watching TV, instead of in the bedroom with you, it will make you feel sad sometimes and glad sometimes; but if the TV is in the **bedroom**, you will be sorry most of the time.

Tighten lids on top of jars, bottles, medicines, fingernail polish, and cosmetics before packing in luggage or putting in purse.

Pills have a "self defense" tactic. They don't think they want to be swallowed. If you drop one, it will hop under a table, roll under a cabinet or fall on a rug that will camouflage it.

❀ ✿ ❀

No matter how often you mention it, your mother-in-law will not leave the thermostat in your home as you set it.

❀ ✿ ❀

"Always tell the **truth**; then you don't have to remember what you said." (I think Mark Twain said that.) Mark Twain is one of my favorite authors. Read his books in school (*Tom Sawyer, Huck Finn,* etc.) and again now for pure pleasure and a better understanding of his talent, humor, genius as he portrays the people and ideas of "the times."

❀ ✿ ❀

Don't throw away what's left of a **baked ham**. The scraps and bone are wonderful to cook in your beans, greens, peas or cabbage. A butcher will cut it into hunks for you; then freeze it and use what you need when you need it. I used some left from Christmas today, and it is June 15.

Everyone should read the **"funny papers."** All are not funny but the ones that are can make your day.

You cannot have too many pairs of **scissors**! Three pairs in the kitchen are not too many—different sizes for different jobs. A pair in the bedroom, office, bathroom—are so "handy." (Pun intended.) A roll of Scotch Tape in all those rooms is also very, very convenient.

Never buy less that 2 pounds of **green beans**. It's not worth cooking fewer than that. Leftovers will keep a week in the fridge and are often better warmed up. The same goes for turnip greens . . . a good mess of greens is at least two big bunches, and you can mix in one bunch of collards or mustard greens, too. Always cook beans and greens in a cast iron pot with lid. They cook better and taste better and are better. (Don't forget fat back, streak of lean or bacon drippings for flavor.)

There is nothing in the world in the **kitchen** better than a good knife, except perhaps two good helping hands. Throw away your dull knives, and buy several sizes of really good ones. They are expensive, but are worth it. Saves much time and temper.

Good **grammar** is always very, very important, no matter who you are, how important you are or how rich you are. The minute you say "between you and I" instead of "between you and me," a person who is well versed in grammar knows that you are <u>not.</u> Also just as bad is "between she and I" instead of "between her and me." To say you "feel badly" means there is something wrong with your sense of touch. If you feel bad, you may be ill or sorry about a friend's accident. No matter how beautiful you are or how expensive your clothes, the minute you say "I am so tired I think I'll lay down," that impression goes out the window. A chicken lays eggs—lay means to put or set. A person lies down (reclines.) Thank goodness for good strict English teachers, Pay attention! Please don't let your answering machine say "we are unable to come to the phone right now." (That could mean your arm is broken or you are not well.)

Pronunciation is extremely important, too. I know I mess up sometimes in this department, but I do say "asked" instead of "axed," February instead of "Feb-you-ary," and library instead of "liberry."

It's also important and helpful to be a good **"speller."** You know I am not, and that's why it makes it so difficult for me to work crossword puzzules . . . puzziles . . . puzzles.

After serving **pot roast** and gravy, use leftovers for hash or vegetable soup (gravy, too).

Rainy days are good days, except too many in a row or on Easter.

Please do not end every **sentence** with "You know what I mean" or "like I said." These and other phrases are over-worked, especially on TV sports shows.

Yard **work** is hard work.

Men love to **holler**, yell and shout, either when they are glad or mad. They like to slam doors and screech off in the car when they are mad. They love to direct traffic, even when it's only standing in the driveway waving their hands to help you back out from a tight spot. (You may have parked crooked.) They can also give you a "look" that melts your heart. Aren't men interesting?

Mexican Egg Bake
(great for brunch-supper)

Preheat Oven to 350 degrees.

- 1 (10 oz.) pkg. cheddar cheese, grated (sharp or mild)
- 1 (10 oz.) pkg. Monterey Jack cheese, grated
- 4 or 5 jalapeño peppers, seeded and chopped very small*
- 5 large eggs, beaten (but not to death)

Grease bottom of Pyrex dish (10X10 or thereabout). Sprinkle bottom with peppers.
Cover peppers with the lightly mixed cheeses.
Pour eggs over everything.
Bake at 350 degrees for 30 minutes.
Cut into serving size (you decide) blocks.

It can remain in dish or (if you serve soon) be arranged on plate. (Pretty garnished with cherry tomatoes.) May substitute 2 small (4 oz.) cans well drained chopped green chili peppers for milder taste*

P.S. When I serve this, people (both men and women) always ask for the recipe—as I did from a friend in Austin, Texas. Garnish with cherry tomatoes.

Having <u>no</u> **flowers** is better than plastic flowers— anywhere! Not on wreaths, in the yard or cemetery. Use fresh flowers to greet guests for luncheons, teas and other celebrations. Arrangements should be loose and natural looking. Not too fixed! (OK—I guess you have to use plastic flowers at the cemetery sometimes.)

❀ ✿ ❀

About **wreaths**: Nothing looks worse on your front door than a bedraggled wreath with faded tattered ribbons. Also, a Christmas wreath after New Year's Day is definitely not appealing nor Christmas decorations either. A grapevine wreath with green vines and fresh flowers is attractive to welcome guests to a party, luncheon or other type of celebration. Also, a basket of fresh flowers on the door is festive and welcoming. Be sure to remove when wilted. Whatever you have should be big enough for the door. <u>No</u> wreath is better than a small, dinky one or a plastic one! I have seen some attractive metal ones that are nice as is or with holly, fruit, vines, flowers, etc., tucked in and around.

❀ ✿ ❀

Empty the bottom rack of the **dishwasher** first. If you do the top first, the water that is still on dishes or in cups, etc. will drip down on bottom dishes.

Makeup is important, especially to such fair ladies as we are. Find the best kind and colors for your skin. Use as much as necessary but not so much as to look like you are using it. In other words, it needs to look as natural as possible. If you had to choose just one item to use, I think blush gives your face the most light, lift and color. Don't wear so much lipstick that it comes off on every cup and napkin. Moisturize, moisturize, moisturize! Learn to apply makeup correctly. Not a dot of blush on each cheek, blend!

Call your mother!!!!

If your **luggage** just will not hold all your stuff, if there are a few more pieces or a pair of shoes, etc., solve your problem with a sack—not just any sack, though. Carry a sack, (surely you have saved one) from Neiman Marcus, Saks Fifth Ave., Ralph Lauren Rodeo Drive. They make an instant statement of impeccable taste and instant acceptance. A grocery bag just will not do—at The Peabody or Ritz.

Fasten your **seat belts** before starting the car! Before I got that smart, I don't know how many mail boxes I barely missed, how many curbs I hit, how often I veered over the center line while trying to fasten that belt as I driving down the road. Dangerous and dumb!!

 Dab on a touch of **lipstick** and a little blush before going into the kitchen to fix breakfast—unless you are fortunate enough to look beautiful when you awake. Your husband will appreciate it, but may not know it!

"Gumption" is something we all have, but sometimes we have to "get it up." If you need to have a luncheon, but just can't get up the "gumption," that means you do not want to clean up the house for a bunch of sharp eyed ladies, do not want to fix the food or clean up afterward. Occasionally a man cannot get up the "gumption" to ask the lady he loves to marry him. That means he thinks she'll say, "No," and break his heart, or say "Yes," and tie him down forever. Sometimes if you really want to get a thing done, you just have to get up the gumption and go full speed ahead.

It is not only hot and uncomfortable but not a good idea to wear **panties** under your panty hose. Actually, it's plain silly. Panty hose <u>are panties</u> with stockings attached. They have a cotton crotch which most "doctors and nurses recommend." (As they say on TV.) I have heard it in doctor's offices. Bacteria thrives in warm, moist, dark places—hence yeast infections, itching, sometimes odor or other problems. Cotton breathes, you need to "air-out." Do not sleep in panties unless you wear a T-shirt or short top. Actually you do not need panties then (just stay under the sheet).

A promise is a **promise**. Don't make one unless you intend to keep it. Promises, sometimes, are hard to keep. A commitment is a commitment. Don't make one unless you can and intend to honor it. Sometimes commitments last longer than promises. More than one million Americans per year break their marriage promises/commitments. A sad state of affairs. A very sad statement.

Thin **pancakes** are better than thick ones.

If you are going to get a **kitten**, take two! There is no way to describe how precious they are playing together. Actually, I think two are less trouble than one, and the cost of feeding is pennies. They keep each other company and are a delight to watch. Also, they are much easier than a puppy or dog— and not as loud—meow, meow!

Often several couples (maybe even 20 or more) host a **large party**. When you leave to attend the social gathering, take the invitation in the car with you so you can review the names of the hosts and hostesses (some you may not even know) to thank for the lovely evening.

This is something you may really want to get your **teeth** into. If they are naturally a pale, creamy shade instead of stark white, it's better to wear ecru or cream colors next to your face instead of white. White shows the contrast with your teeth. However, now with the whitening products available at drug stores and groceries plus, bleaching at the dentist you have the opportunity to have white, pearly teeth, too.

Free and delightful **"sachets"** are in many high class (and high price) clothing magazines and enclosed with bills from high-end department stores (Neiman's, Saks). They are the perfumed strips of paper (advertisements) that can easily be torn off and tucked in your underwear or sleepwear drawers. Mostly I just put them in shoes in my closet or on a shelf (not touching silk). Your closet will have a light, fresh fragrance. It is not strong enough to cling to your clothes or interfere with your own perfume. Five or more at one time is not too many. They are not long lasting so throw some away when you add others. It is OK to "litter" with nice fragrances.

As you have heard, the Lord gave us five senses, but **smart people**, through experience, acquired two more . . . horse and common. Some have even added another they call "Street Smart." If you have the above mentioned plus taste, smell, sight, hearing and touch, you are a wise and lucky girl.

If you **borrow** something, return it as soon as possible in same or better condition. Do not borrow clothes or other personal items (combs, lipstick, etc.) or lend them. Just say, "I have germs." Do not borrow any breakable item unless you are certain you can replace it.

It is difficult to find your glasses if you do not have them on.

I think of all our "modern conveniences," **indoor plumbing** is the most wonderful. With just the touch of your hand you can have hot or cold water or flush a commode. (Next best is with the flick of the thermostat— you get heat when you are cold and cool air when you are hot.)

Yes, I save **coupons**, and have for years. (I used to even save green stamps.) Now however, I only save them worth 50 cents or more. Saving money is a deed I owe my family and my hard working husband. When I finally decide to use a coupon, I go through the file and discover that most of them are now out of date. These I throw away. The others I save to throw away next time.

Don't ask me why, but it's easier to **count** to 10 twice than 20 all at once. Want to touch your toes 20 times? Do it 10 times twice. No sweat!

Men can make you happy and sad, mad or glad, thrilled or disappointed. They can be gentle, sweet and loving. They can give you their heart or break yours. There's an old song, "A Good Man Is Hard To Find." If you find one, take good care of him, and try to make him happy.

When making **muffins**, don't beat the batter. Just moisten the ingredients gently.

Sometimes things that seem like a **catastrophe** at the moment, work out for the best in the long run. Ask yourself, "Will it really matter in five years?" (Or next week!)

If you plan to have **company**, don't let anyone spray the house for bugs or lay new flooring or paint, etc. that day. There's always an odor (perhaps not too unpleasant), but still an odor that lingers 12 to 24 hours or longer.

It is better to get the **jelly** in the peanut butter than to get the peanut butter in the jelly.

Therefore, when making peanut butter and jelly sandwiches, put the jelly on the bread first. Then add peanut butter. A little jelly never harms the taste of peanut butter, but a little peanut butter in the jelly jar can overpower the taste of jelly—and is NOT a welcome surprise on your hot biscuits at breakfast.

Do not add salt to any **kraut dish** (pepper OK) or one that calls for soy sauce. Both are already plenty salty.

Cuss! Cuss! Cuss! Seems that some people (not just men) cannot open their mouths without a cuss word—even when they are not mad. Probably they think that adding curse words makes what they are saying seem more important. Wrong! Maybe they think curse words will make you pay closer attention. Wrong! Actually they <u>detract</u> from what they are trying to say. Could it be that curse words make them think that we think they are important? Wrong! Probably their vocabulary does not contain adequate adjectives to describe what they are trying to communicate. Possibly they do not know what an adjective is. Horror of horrors, it could be they were raised in a home where trashy curse words were the everyday language.

Now, we hear **bad words** on all TV programs and movies, and read them in books, everyday. They have lost their "Pow!" "Pow!" is what happened when Clark Gable said, "Frankly, my dear, I don't give a damn!" in *Gone with the Wind*. The whole world gasped. It was daring, it was delightful! It was swearing, but not trashy. Anyone who goes to church hears a lot of hell and damnation—but the "F" word and others are not acceptable in nice company— or in your mouth or in your ears. Between men, or among a group of men, it might be OK because it makes them feel bigger, more important and manly. So be it! (Sometimes throwing in a "damn or hell" might make YOU feel better, but not when the children are around.) Enough about that.

❀ ❀ ❀

When a friend has a new **baby** or has moved into another house, save your visit until several weeks later (unless you are bringing food!) Then, do not stay long!

❀ ❀ ❀

I can't stress often enough: When you have a **club meeting**, etc., in the daytime at your house, have a dinner party (etc.) that night. Your house is already clean, with flowers, etc.,—or if you have too many to entertain at once, have one two nights in a row. The food doesn't have to be the same, but it's easier if it is. The correct dishes, glasses, etc., will already be ready.

Always use good **manners**. It doesn't cost anything and usually pays off. Do not lower yourself to bad manners. Always be a "lady"—not just a woman. Every lady is a woman; but every woman is not a lady.

 Don't sit down in any **bathroom** until you have checked to make sure toilet tissue is available. How terrible to discover too late that there is not any.

Any potatoes can be used to make **potato salad**. Red, white or yellow potatoes hold their shape better. Russet, the type used most often to bake, tend to be crumbly and drier, more like mashed potatoes when tossed to make salad.

Sexual attitudes change with age.

Try not to have a **doctor's** appointment on Friday for teeth, glasses, contacts, etc. If something goes wrong (toothache, contacts do not fit properly, medicine makes you sick or you have a reaction), it is often difficult to get hold of the doctor on Friday night—or Saturday or Sunday.
Best days for appointments are Monday, Tuesday, and Wednesday.

You are very **lucky** to have the father you have. He has never begrudged one penny spent on you for doctors, medicine, glasses, dentist, camps, Christmas, birthdays, clothes, school activities—never does he complain about how much money you are costing him—only when he sees things needlessly wasted or carelessly abused or lost does he get riled up—and I don't blame him.

Potatoes baked in your oven have better taste and texture than those fixed in your microwave. Takes longer, but is well worth it!

This works for both **tomatoes and peaches**. For easy peeling, plunge them into boiling water for about 30 seconds or more. Remove with a slotted spoon and drop into cold water. The skins slip off easily when they are cool enough to handle.

This morning while walking on the treadmill and watching TV, I learned that **rubber bands** will last longer if kept in the refrigerator. Now who, pray tell, has room in their refrigerator for rubber bands? And if you put them in there, how would you ever find them? My rubber bands last long enough on the kitchen doorknob, and I can always find the correct size.

My easiest recipe

Parched Peanuts

(Nuts to you) Delicious, good for you, and easy to do.

Preheat oven to 500 degrees. Spread raw peanuts in the shell all over (one layer) a large baking pan with ½ inch or more turned up edge. About 16 to 20 ounces according to the size of the pan. Place peanuts in oven. Immediately turn oven OFF!! Let peanuts remain in oven until cool. Enjoy!!

It's fun to shell peanuts and pop them into your mouth. "You can't eat just one." But deciding where to put the shells is a problem. Have a big bowl or wastebasket handy. Keep peanuts away from little children until you are sure they can handle them. Even adults can choke on nuts.

Note: Dry roasted peanuts have less calories. Nuts are high in fat, but mainly the "good" kind. They can replace grains or red meats in your diet. Eating nuts at least five times a week cut women's risk of developing type 2 (adult-onset) diabetes by about 30% reports Harvard's school of public health researchers.

P.S. By the way, peanuts ARE NOT really nuts. They are legumes, in the bean family.

Again, I repeat . . . no matter how often you mention it, your mother-in-law will not leave the **thermostat** in your home as you set it.

A **sweater** is a wonderful garment to have with you— especially at an airport, in a restaurant or hospital, even in some grocery stores. Anytime of the year you may wish for one. It's amazing to me how inexperienced mothers take their precious, young babies to these places barefooted and sleeveless. (I wonder if they are the same moms who have their tender-skinned toddlers at the beach with no hat or sunscreen.) Perhaps they do have on sunscreen lotion and are just naturally that pink color!

When **stockings** are on sale, buy a good supply of all colors you will need.

If you use **liquid make-up base**, put it on stark naked. If you wait until you are in your underwear, you will be sorry because a drop will always get on your bra or panties, and it is difficult to wash out. I have also gotten it on nightgown, robe and other clothing, even when trying to be very careful.

There is no need to **fear**, but sometime it will seem to saturate your mind. Don't let it. (Joshua 1:9) "Be strong and of good courage; be not afraid . . . for the Lord God is with you wherever you go"; and (Psalm 27:1) "the Lord is my light and my salvation, whom shall I fear? The Lord is the strength of my life, of whom shall I be afraid?"

Brush your teeth right after supper, and then you will not be so tempted to eat again before bedtime. Well, you may be tempted but might hesitate.

If at all possible, do not plan on going out on the evening that you return home from a **trip**. You will be too tired, too rushed and wish you could stay home. Also, try not to make any appointments for the day after you return from your trip. You will need that time to unwind, unpack, catch-up on mail, etc. (A hair appointment will help you to relax and make you look better.)

When you **lose something**, look where you think it is, and if it is not there—look where you think it is not and it is (often).

An **arrangement** for your breakfast table or in the kitchen can easily be made of fresh fruit or vegetables. The vegetable one is attractive with cabbage, eggplant, squash, onions (green ones are nice with roots and long leaves), avocados and tomatoes. A bunch of radishes with leaves look pretty. A fruit one is colorful with bananas, apples, grapes, peaches, lemons, limes, and perhaps a grapefruit or cantaloupe, or just a big bowl or tray of apples or lemons and limes. These arrangements are easy and much cheaper than flowers. Plus you can eat them! A pretty colander or a big wooden bowl make charming containers.

Take good care of your **skin** . . . all over . . . especially in the sun. Use sunscreen, hats, and sunglasses for protection. Your skin never forgets! The older you get the more your skin shows former sun abuse.

The **Secret** to forming stiff peaks quickly with whipping cream: Chill beaters and bowl before whipping, and make sure cream is cold. Opposite is true with egg whites. They beat up better at room temperature. When right out of the fridge, put them in warm water for a minute or two. Be sure not to have even a speck of yellow in it!

Don't ever buy the ugly **furniture** that has the "legs" covered with fabric.

There is a place for lovely **silk flowers**, but I do not have one. They can complement the colors in a room and are often very expensive, but still, they are artificial. They demand little (dusting) care, but can add no life to a room. Dried flowers can be attractive. Spend your money and time on live plants and flowers. If they die, buy new ones (they are still cheaper than silk), and never, never leave dead ones in a room. (I think I can hear howls from silk flower lovers, florists and decorators.) Walking into an office that is "decorated" with dying plants gives a very bad impression. Better no plants at all. These offices are also the ones with magazines three years old.

When you are feeling low and blue and tired, you need a chocolate **transfusion**.

When attending one of your children's **ball games**, be encouraging. Do not criticize any of the players. (You may be sitting in front of their mother) or the referee. You may scowl (gently) at shouters of derogatory remarks or roll your eyes.

Try not to **schedule** any workmen to lay carpet, do yard work, etc., on a Friday. They will be in too much of a hurry or might leave before finishing to start their weekend.

When you **make a deal** with carpenters, plumbers, electricians, etc., be sure they understand that they are to stay at your house on the job until they are finished. If you don't, they will often leave to go to another unfinished job or start a new one. Just tell them not to start unless they are ready to stay until it is completed. If you don't, you are likely to find your house in a mess for several days instead of several hours.

When you buy something at the **grocery** already prepared (smoked chicken, casseroles, slaw, etc.), put it in one of your dishes as soon as you get home. It looks much more appealing and more "homemade" than in the foil pan, plastic, or whatever it came in. Your family will think you prepared it when they open the fridge. . . .

FEED THE BIRDS!

If you have a maid or **housekeeper** who is dependable, honest, clean, has no small children, tries to please, is pleasant, rarely uses the telephone, has her own transportation, does not smoke in your home, has common sense, needs the job—PAY HER WELL! Usually they are over 40. (I know college graduates who have little common sense. You do not learn that in school!)

Compromise is an important ingredient of a happy marriage. Remember, you are not perfect either, nor can you be right all the time.

A great pick-me-up (for after lunch) is a little lie-down, first chance you get. There is nothing like a little **nap** to revive you for the afternoon and evening. Rest no less than 30 minutes and no longer than one hour. More makes you grumpy and groggy for a while when you awake. A nap will put you in a better mood at suppertime (which is often stressful for a tired mom trying to feed a hungry family). We used to call it the "witching" hour, because I turned into a witch after working all day and coming home with so many more jobs to do. Yes, I know everyone cannot take time for a nap, but some big companies are suggesting a short "rest time" (even while at your desk) after lunch. New moms need to nap when the baby does. Take your phone off the hook and put a sign on your front door.

The **older** I get, the older "OLD" is.

It's so nice when men put the **toilet seat** down, but don't nag if they forget. However, they should always remember when to put the toilet seat up (a wet seat is unforgivable) and flush.

No matter if you drink several cups of **coffee** during the day, none tastes as good as the first one in the morning.

Some parents say, "Don't do as I do, but do as I say do." Please never repeat that. Your **children** will learn much more from what you do than what you say. Remember that!

A house cannot have too many closets, bathrooms or bookcases.

If you are **walking or jogging** on a road, always face the traffic. Walk on your left side. That way, you can see a car approaching and not look back to see if one is coming up behind you. My mother taught me that when I was young, and everybody did it. Now it seems nobody told half of the roadrunners and walkers, and they do not have sense enough to figure it out. I've heard that this may be illegal. If it is, it seems stupid to me. What do you think????

Do not build on a lot that has no **privacy** in back, such as a street all around. It puts your whole yard and you on view to the world. A good neighborhood is as important (perhaps more) as a good house. Build as far away from traffic and noise as possible.

> **Praise** your husband often in the presence of others.

If a man (young or old) **hits** you (or your children) in anger or rage, leave him at once and do not go back or see him again. He will never get better, just worse.

Sometimes (usually after age 40), some men suddenly decide to **"act young"** so no one (female) will think they're getting old. Men who have previously shunned nightlife suddenly must dance every dance—preferably with "sweet young things."

These men try to **"dress younger"** and wear a youthful hair style—if they have any hair. The ones bald on top let hair grow long around the edges and hang over their collar or brush it carefully over the bald part and spray it down. Both styles are obvious and distasteful. They buy a sports car, if possible, and find "reasons" to attend meetings, gathering, games, parties where young ladies may be who will listen attentively to what they say and let them give a "fatherly" hug or pat here and there. It doesn't seem to dawn on them that this special attention they're basking in comes along with their paying the bill—for food, drinks, transportation, etc., etc. At this time, they will probably find an excuse not to wear their wedding ring because it "is too tight" or "messes up their golf swing or tennis grip."

This "act young" **malady** strikes more men in their fifties than any other age group. Even staid "family men" seem to succumb. Sometimes a divorce is the result, but often the wife holds on until he wears himself out and realizes that a slower pace (and a lower credit card balance!) in his own age group is much more comfortable. He never believes that his money is what bought his "fling" and is content to think that his personality, charm, and looks kept the ladies enthralled— (those ladies who were glad to have a "ticket" to food, drinks, entertainment, gifts and escort services plus a shoulder to cry on, free advice, financial help, and sympathy if they needed it.)

I really don't always blame the "ladies." It is still a **man's world**—(no matter if we have come a long way, baby) and the easiest way to get ahead—or whatever you want—is to flatter the waning ego of a man who is suddenly not so sure of his masculine power and thinks he may have "missed out" on something along the way. Don't ever let yourself think that this cannot happen to your husband.

The "act young" malady can affect **older women**, too, but not nearly as often. Too much makeup, too much hair color, too many visits to the plastic surgeon, style of clothes too young, etc. They flirt and giggle outrageously and seem silly and pitiful. I am sorry they are so desperate.

Boys of 15 or 50 will only "go as far as they think you will let them." Be careful and do not **tease**! Be sure someone always knows whom you are with and where.

Twin beds and bunk beds are good for children only. **Two double beds** are the best bet for husband and wife. Both of you will sleep much better: so always try and have your bedroom big enough to accommodate two big beds or a king-sized. Actually, separate but adjoining double beds would be ideal. (In spite of the cons, the pros outweigh them.) Of course this comes only after several years of marriage.

Lord Byron said "Man's love is of man's life a thing apart; 'tis woman's whole existence." Think about it.

Hand out **gift certificates** for free burgers at McDonald's, Wendy's, etc., to homeless people on street corners, etc. (explain to them what it is—FREE.) They cannot spend it on drugs, etc. and your children will know you are showing concern.

In this day and time, ashtrays may become **collectors' items**. Use the pretty ones to hold change or earrings on your dresser, to catch dripping candle wax, or as coasters for iced tea. (They do not have to match.) All my silver-rimmed ones were wedding gifts, so they could be called antiques now.

> Darlings, you should definitely practice the art of **diplomacy** which is letting someone have it your way.

This I admit. I seem to get more comfort and strength and joy from singing and/or reading from our church **hymnal** than from reading from my Bible. Of course, I know all the songs of praise, of hope and joy originated from the Bible. It's just that the verses are so easy to read and the music puts the words and songs in my heart. Most were written so long ago about words and happenings and promises made even longer ago, and still, after hundreds and hundreds and hundreds of years, the Bible words lifted up in song, lift us up also.

Do not let **water** run while brushing teeth. Hundreds of gallons of water can be saved this way.

Doctors now realize that worry and anxiety can be as disabling as physical limitations. Either can limit us or even prevent us from functioning. Either or both can make us physically ill or mentally and emotionally disabled. "Be not anxious about tomorrow because tomorrow will be anxious for itself. Let the day's own troubles be sufficient for the day." (Matthew 6:34) When we are overly anxious about the future, the present moment can be ruined. Dwelling on the past is unproductive; it cannot be changed. "Let not your heart be troubled, neither be afraid." (John 14:1) These are wonderful words, but sometimes hard to obey.

If you're meeting someone at the **airport**, call before leaving home and check on the time of flight arrival. Often it is delayed and you will have a long wait at the airport unless you know the new expected arrival time.

All three of you took **music lessons**, piano, flute, clarinet; but the lessons didn't take. Well, you did learn to read music, play a little piano, but the best lesson you learned is to appreciate those who can really play an instrument. I am sorry to say I did the same thing, but I never learned to play as well as you.

After a **wedding** in your immediate family, have someone gather the candles from the church and reception. You paid for them, and they will come in handy some other time. Also, if there is a lot of food leftover from the reception (or any other occasion) have it packaged for your refrigerator or freezer. You have paid for it. Use it later or give it to someone who would enjoy it. Ten years after our girls' weddings, I used some of the candles at two different dinner parties and still have many remaining. Just be sure to store them in a cool place.

Worth quoting from Victor Hugo: "Have courage for the greatest sorrows of life and patience for the smaller ones; and when you have laboriously accomplished your daily tasks, go to sleep in peace, God is awake."

Everyone needs to **"work with the public"** at least once—as a waitress, clerk, salesperson, office personnel, etc. It's an experience you won't forget, and it may change your attitude, understanding and perspective about people in high or low places.

I wish my friends would tell me when I have **lipstick** on my teeth.

Decorating the house will never be as important to your husband as it is to you. It's just not in their understanding to spend money in that department. Therefore, find another way—save for it, have your own checking account, or introduce him to a beautiful decorator. She'll sell him!!!

> Display your children's favorite art and schoolwork.

The **best gift** you can give your children is to love your husband.

Remember, were it not for your **"wonderful"** mother-in-law, you wouldn't have your wonderful husband.

Teachers, umpires, and **policemen** are always "right." So don't argue, even though they may be wrong. (You'll lose, probably.) Life is not always fair.

Life is not fair. It is full of **problems**—especially for teenagers. Acne is one problem that is embarrassing to them and causes poor self-esteem. Help them have one less problem. Take them to a dermatologist.

To have a **happy** friend, take a dessert, salad or casserole to her for no special reason.

Whenever your husband asks you to go on a **trip** with him—Go!!!!

Put any **flowers** your child brings you in a pretty vase— even if it's a weed.

When you buy sugar, flower, meal, etc., make sure the package is not punctured or torn anywhere and seal is secure . . . else you may find a slow trickle of the ingredients in the bottom of your **grocery bag** . . . or worse, a pile on your pantry shelf (maybe weevils, too).

The shorter your **hair** the more important your eyes and eye makeup. Too, with short hair, you can just "give it a lick and a promise" and go! (You do need to have a good cut.)

Try to take lots of **pictures** of your third and fourth, etc., child and save some of their "art work," letters from camp, etc., even if you have to pile them in a box instead of a baby book (as you did your first two), because those last children will complain forever when they realize that you have hundreds of mementos of the older children, but fewer, (a lot fewer) of their childhood. Only after they have children will the same thing (no time, too much to do, etc.) happen to them. It is too late for me. I have been hearing sad comments about this forever, but there must be some compensation for the youngest, because you older girls say we spoiled the baby—we let her get away with all the things you couldn't do. I don't deny that we were more lax (but not on all the things). Perhaps we learned along the way that some things were probably OK (others absolutely not)—besides, we were tired.

Creams and lotions

in tubes are very difficult to get out when the product is almost used up. Take scissors and cut tube in half. It is easy to get to all that remains, and that's always about 20 percent. As expensive as cosmetics are, that's a big savings.

When making an **appointment** with your doctor, ask to be the first patient he sees. That way, you (or your children) don't have to wait in his office because he is three or four patients behind. Of course, there may be other reasons for his being late.

Keep a **calendar** by all your telephones, one large enough to write on by your bed (desk) and in the kitchen.

> **Always turn cold water on first and hot water off first.**

When you pack away your **shoes** until the next season (of summer or winter), take those that need heels fixed, repairs or just polishing to the cobbler and get them all ready to be worn before you put them away. Then months later, when you need them, they will be ready and looking good. Some may need to be discarded.

The shape of the cup is very important, I think, when selecting **china**. The handle should be large enough for your finger to hold comfortably, and the total design be pleasing, not just the pattern. Food seems to look better on a plate that is not "too busy" with a pattern.

I declare that I think some girls are **catty** and conniving from the cradle to the grave. Usually they are jealous of your hair, your grades, your clothes, your boy friend, your girl friends, whatever. It's better to have them as friends than enemies—but best to avoid them whenever possible. They can cause trouble!!!

Hold your head and shoulders up when walking. Do not slouch. You may not be a queen, but you can walk like one.

Never have your **picture** taken while holding a drink (beer or alcohol). It's not ladylike—at any age, anywhere, and certainly never with a cigarette. When your picture is being taken, make sure your feet are not closer to the camera than you are (they will look huge), hands, too. Never chew gum in public . . . a rule we learned at Ward Belmont. Do not dance holding a drink or cigarette. (Don't bother to smoke anyway.)

If possible have your **carport** or garage not facing the same way as your front door—and not facing the street.

It is a **wonderful feeling** to have the kitchen clean and the dishwasher and washing machine "going" and a pound cake in the freezer.

Always pack an extra bra, panties, and stockings.

Most cans of **powdered cleanser** (Comet, Ajax, etc.) have six or more holes in the top covered with a seal. When you remove the seal, leave about half of the holes covered (replace seal or do not completely remove). Your cleaner will last longer or you won't waste it by using more than needed as most of us usually do. Also, add water to your dishwasher liquid when it is about three-quarters full and shake and it will last 25 percent longer.

Don't buy a cheap **water hose**. It will kink up and drive you crazy. Buy the best you can get—no kink or kink resistant. It will last longer , and so will your patience . . . except that <u>it will still catch</u> on every corner, knob, tire, invisible stump, etc., etc., etc.

Buy **brown sugar** in a plastic bag—stays soft better than in a box.

When talking on the **telephone** about any type of business, always get the name of the person to whom you are speaking. Then, if you need any follow up of the conversation, you'll have a name to ask for or refer to. This includes making reservations, ordering, etc.

When your husband comes home from work and immediately asks you what you are making for dinner, tell him (if you are worn out from your day) **"reservations."** Of course this is something only to do once in a while. Got this thought from one of my good California friends. (If he is worn out, have mercy and take something from the freezer or order out.)

Don't learn (or at least pretend you can't) to use an **outside grill** or lawn mower. That way your husband will always have to do it and will be a great help. It will give him a specialty . . . and if he won't grill, he will at least pay someone to cut the grass.

When you hear "nik-click, nik-click, nik-click" under the **car hood**, have oil and fan belt checked. Usually you need oil. It also can be speedometer or hole in exhaust. (Well, maybe.)

Keep using **three toothbrushes**, not exactly alike. This way you don't use a damp brush and different brushes fit different places on your teeth. Brush gums gently at least once a day. Throw brush away after you have been ill.

A plant or bush makes a nice **housewarming** gift. Also bulbs.

Always use your very best **toilet paper** in your guest bathroom. Sometimes you are judged by your toilet paper, especially if it is cheap.

When building your **house**, be sure that your main clothes closets are vented and air conditioned, else the closet will eventually smell musty and like worn shoes.

Be sure to wear a very **good bra** when horseback riding or playing tennis, or else you will contribute to sagging breasts, which certainly makes you look older. Most of your breasts is soft, fatty tissue and breaks down easily—so take good care of your figure and provide proper support for your breasts. You will look younger—longer.

Since my daughter Candy's death, I have not really been afraid of **dying**, and I am convinced we will all be together again someday "JOYOUSLY"! I am sure.

> There is a lot of **comfort** to be found in the arms of a man who loves you.

Remember always **"Who you are."** This sage advice has been handed down to us all from your grandmother (Nonnie) for years. . . . Remembering who you are in all situations will clear many a troubling temptation from your life. If you're not sure . . . ask your parents! Remember you are a <u>representative</u> of your family.

Have about two **special toys** kept near (but out of reach) of the telephone. Then when you are on the phone, and your toddler keeps bothering you, give him the "special toy," one at a time, for a few minutes of uninterrupted conversation.

 Wash **strawberries** right before capping. This keeps from washing away good juices and taste.

When staying at the **hospital** with a relative or friend . . . always take a sweater; even in July—hospital rooms often seem cool. Some nurses will have on a cardigan. If spending the night on a cot in the room, take a pretty quilt or afghan to spread on top. There is no way to make up a cot and have it look nice; so covering it hides all the wrinkles. Also, the warmth and weight make it feel good at night—plus it adds a little of "home" and color to the room. Do not hesitate to ask nurses for whatever you need and thank them. You are charged for every little thing, so take home anything you can use, even if it is a half-empty box of Kleenex.

One grandmother-friend of mine told me she tried to childproof her house, but they keep getting in anyway.

Order **bulbs** for fall planting in the spring or summer (they will be shipped at planting time) and pay by credit card. Do any Christmas shopping you can early (summer) and pay for the gifts. That way, all is paid for well before the "heavy" fall, winter, and Christmas shopping begins. Also, bulbs make good gifts for friends who love their yard and gardens.

Often when your **feelings** are hurt, you will think of saying and doing many things to retaliate or get revenge. You may be awake all night thinking of it, or spend most of the day with it on your mind. My advice is—don't say or do it. If you will wait 24 hours, something will happen to make you glad you didn't say or do what you thought of.

> Never leave a **baby** in a room to "cry it out." They need the closeness of you, your understanding and patience. Do not punish a child by making him go to bed. Bed should not be associated with punishment.

Do not **fuss** at a child for waking you in the night—for water or bad dreams, or any reason. Soothe him, calm him. You will get back to sleep much quicker and so will the child. Doing this is not always easy. Don't punish a child who is slow to potty train or for "accidents." Be patient, please.

Light fixtures: Buy your bulbs when you buy your light fixtures. Often the correct size is difficult to find. Make sure the bulbs are available before paying for the fixtures.

Best Spoon Bread
(oh so good!)

Preheat oven to 375 degrees

- 1½ cup light cream (I have used skim milk or 2 percent with good results.)
- ½ cup white cornmeal (have used plain or self rising with good results)
- 3 tablespoons butter or oleo (stick, not soft)
- 3 eggs separated (yokes in small bowl, whites in bowl for beating)
- ½ teaspoon of salt

Grease a 1 quart casserole (Pam OK). HEAT milk in heavy pan over medium heat—do not boil. When hot, slowly POUR cornmeal in it stirring until smooth (or almost). REMOVE from heat, continue stirring and ADD salt and butter. MIX well. ADD egg yokes 1 at a time and stir in. Beat egg whites until stiff. Slowly and gently FOLD egg whites into mixture. Pour into casserole dish or four cup souffle bowl. SMOOTH over top. BAKE 30 minutes or until top is golden brown. SERVE at once with or without extra butter.

P.S. This serves 4 people, but Doug and I eat it all!! Good with a green or fruit salad.

If when roasting a nice piece of meat, you take it out of the oven and serve it at once, congratulations—you just ruined that beautiful meat. Start slicing right after cooking, and you get a big pool of juice on the plate. The meat tastes dry and tough. It needs to **rest** 5 to 10 minutes before serving. The rest makes your meat juicy and tender. Also remember, just because you have removed something from the heat, does not mean it has finished cooking. Food-science experts can explain the whys of it; but what matters is the <u>rest</u> is up to you, and it's important to the taste and tenderness.

> **Never ever consider the companionship of a man (or woman) who is not considerate of animals or children. I do not mean that they have to love them, but they should be careful not to mistreat them or hurt their feelings. Never trust anyone who will carelessly hurt a child or an animal.**

The showing of hot and heavy affection in public is definitely a NO NO; certainly in **bad taste,** actually rude and crude. There is a time and place for everything, and that is not it. No exceptions!

No matter how often you mention it, your **mother-in-law** will not leave the thermostat in your home as you set it. (You know I am talking about me.)

Teach your children to make a **choice** when someone asks them if they prefer one thing or another—such as "Would you like a Coke or a Sprite?" Tell them not to say, "I don't care."

One advantage of **getting older** is you have more leeway. Aging gives you "permission" . . . but not to be rude.

What to have for **supper** is the constant question that lingers in your mind daily (wherever you go, or whatever you are doing). It will be nag, nag, nag until you've decided. There is no escape.

Seen on church sign:
"Forbidden fruit makes many jams."

Beware of **driving** behind a man who is wearing a hat—a real, honest-to-goodness hat (like Elliot Ness). You will poke along at 20 miles per hour behind a car with no blinkers or one blinker that stays on the whole time. However, he is probably a nice old gentleman and someone's grandfather; but he still drives at one speed—S-L-O-W-L-Y. Same for old ladies whose heads you can't even see. (I fear I'm in the fast lane on the way to S-L-O-W-L-Y. I promise to sit on a pillow so you can see my head.)

"Togetherness . . ." The romance will last much longer if each of you has the privacy of your own bathroom and bed. . . . Bed hopping is OK. (Yes, I understand this is not always possible. Also, it may not be desired til you have been married for quite a while.)

> **Rock** your child as long as he or she will let you, even 'til 6 or 7 years of age. The closeness is good for both of you. Let older ones sit in your lap. This time will pass too soon.

Try and do all your **personal grooming** when he is not present, putting on makeup, hair combing, doing your nails. No boy likes to be with a girl who is <u>constantly</u> repairing makeup or rearranging her clothes and <u>fixing</u> her hair.

Keep the top of your **dresser** or vanity uncluttered, (even if the drawers are stuffed full). Hair pens, spilled powder, open eye shadow boxers all look messy and detract from your image indicating that all your attractiveness is just artificial. Keep extra razors, feminine products, etc. all out of sight. Perfumes and bath oils, however, seem to be a pleasant, female sight to men so leave them in view.

A child can eat a good supper, go to bed, and wake up in a few hours with a **terrible ear pain**. Very likely there will not be any fever. Do all you can to comfort him and take him to a doctor as soon as possible even though pain seems to be gone.

Even if you don't want to, make the effort, whatever it takes, to go to **church** every Sunday. You will always find it was well worth it. Your soul and spirit need food just as much as your body does. Though you may not feel the need before church, you will always feel filled and refreshed afterwards (even with a poor sermon or preacher).

Do not go to **Florida** in January thru April expecting warm, pretty weather. It will be cloudy, wet and cool. Some days 4-6 hours of sun may shine—but not while you are there, unless it's the day you arrive or the day you leave. (This problem can probably be solved by going to the most southern part of the state.)

Try not to use dark wood **furniture** in a sunny room because no matter how often you dust it, it will look dusty and be dusty also. It really will show up. Painted furniture, wicker, etc., are best in a sunny room.

Every time I call the **dry cleaners** to indicate that they have left something out of my delivery, I look in my closet and find it hanging under something.

If you are staying with someone in the **hospital**, wear quiet shoes, (not hard heels), do not hit or jar the bed (don't sit on it either), don't feel like you must talk all the time, do not wear lots of perfume, do not keep the TV on unless they ask for it and never have it loud. If visitors come (several at a time), find an excuse to leave the room a few minutes so they can talk privately without your hanging around . . . and if they stay too long, discreetly mention that the patient tires easily. If they don't leave, don't be discreet.

If you pack **lunches**, save the little salt and pepper packages they serve you on planes or at fast-food restaurants. They come in handy.

A list of **people** who have entertained you is good to have. If it seems difficult to keep . . . at least put it on your calendar, and maybe you can refer to it if you save it. It may help keep you from leaving someone out you really need and want to entertain.

Nothing is prettier or sweeter by a brick (shady) wall or walk than **violets and Lily of the Valley**. Hyacinths are nice, too, but not in a row. Arrange in groups of 3 to 5.

Wherever you live, make friends with the family of a **good doctor** or dentist. It is good to know these people, not only business-wise, but personally. Never call on them after business hours for personal attention unless absolutely necessary and then make it clear that it is necessary. . . .

A written **"thank you"** is always appreciated, no matter how brief. (Nice stationery is a wise investment.) Never hesitate to show appreciation for a favor, however small, in the most immediate way you can—a smile, a word, a gift, a touch, a call, a hug—whatever seems appropriate. You can't say "thank you" too many times or too many ways.

Any **meat** you buy at the grocery such as ham, smoked chicken, turkey, etc. (whole) needs to be cooked some more to taste really "done"—about 45 minutes to 60 minutes at 350 degrees for a ham and 30 to 45 minutes for turkey or chicken depending on size. This keeps them from being so slick. Also, have them half it while frozen at the grocery unless you need to serve the whole at one time. Halves are easier to store and use later.

If possible get to know your **pharmacist**, and let your pharmacist get to know you. This is easier said than done—much easier in a small town than a city. If you have all your prescriptions filled at the same place, possible bad drug interaction can be avoided. Make sure your doctor is aware of all drugs and medications you are taking.

Use good **manners** at all times. It does not cost anything, and usually pays big dividends. Do not lower yourself to bad manners. . . .

> There is only one kind of **minor operation** and that is the one not being performed on you!

People should <u>earn</u> or merit **reward**—not receive it as a handout—because they are too lazy to work. It is not right to take away from those who work and give it to those who refuse to work or help themselves. In the long run, this causes low self-esteem in those doing the receiving, and resentment in those doing the giving. Of course, those who are sick or disabled need help, and we should always take care of and help children.

If you are ever really **"rich,"** let the wealth make yourself and others happy. Provide your family with many **opportunities** (not just things) to travel, to study, to experience—skiing, sailing, fishing, good visits to foreign countries, art, good music, etc.

Build a **children's hospital**—all patient rooms on the ground floor—all sound proof, all with windows placed low so that a child in bed can look outside. Construct the building in a U shape, and inside the U have a lake with ducks, flower gardens, trees with bird houses and other interesting things to watch—squirrels, chipmunks, etc. Have a mobile aquarium of pretty fish that can be put in a child's room. Watching them is soothing and interesting. Have caged birds that may be put in a child's room. They are attractive and amusing. (Perhaps some of these ideas are not feasible, just wishful thinking.)

The most beautiful music is not determined by the size of the **organ**, but by the expertise of the player. (Think on that.)

A grand time for a **big party** is the first or second week in November before Thanksgiving. People are getting in a holiday mood and will not be "tired" of holiday parties. Also, your menu will be easier to plan as folks will not yet be stuffed with holiday foods. Too, they will welcome the chance to wear their new party clothes, or have a reason to go ahead and buy some.

A **commitment** made in the heat of the moment may tend to cool off as time goes by. Think ahead! (with your head, not being influenced by other body parts).

> Learn from the **mistakes** of others. There is not enough time to make them all yourself. Mistakes are good teachers.

If you are **overweight**, try to lose it; too skinny, try to add it. Seems like that would be an eating pleasure, but have read that it's just as difficult to add as to subtract. Difficult to believe.

How to be a cool and smooth **operator**:

Peeling hard **boiled eggs** can be an easy and slippery job. Just cool the eggs in cold water right after cooking. (You can even put some ice in the water.) Then crack the shells in lots of places. As you hold the eggs under running water, just slip off the shell for a smooth egg.

Before **icing a cake**, make sure it is completely cool. Even a slightly warm cake will make the icing drip and run. A cool cake helps the icing to go on smoothly, not so many crumbs.

There are four **"best smells"** in the kitchen—bacon frying, coffee perking, onions and bell peppers sautéing and a cake in the oven.

❀ ✿ ❀

Dear ones, anything plus **bacon** equals a winner. If I could have only one meat in my life, I think I would choose bacon. You can serve it with eggs, sprinkled on casseroles and salads, BLT or wrapped around olives, mushrooms, etc. Bacon drippings enhance the flavor of green beans, other vegetables and soups. Yes, if I had to be restricted to just one meat, bacon would be the survivor. (We are not going to mention f-a-t because that is what makes it taste so good. Sometimes you just have to forget that three-letter word.) . . .

❀ ✿ ❀

Read a lot—Learn a lot.

❀ ✿ ❀

Frozen cookies and cakes are good to eat—I mean they are good to eat <u>frozen</u>. I discovered this because I put cookies, cakes, and candies in the freezer to "hide from myself and keep them unavailable." However, a sweet attack cannot be ignored, and so I attacked the hoard. Couldn't even wait to use the micro. Oh, how sweet it is—frozen!—(except the candy is sometimes too hard).

For a really **"big show"** in your yard and garden, plant Coleus. There are many varieties, and they are pretty planted together. They do fine in shade or semi-shade but will take bright sun. Water often. They love heat. A big urn planted with coleus in the middle and ivy or something hanging over the rim is striking. Much reward for little work. Don't skimp, use plenty of plants. Pinch off the blooms for bushy plant.

An aching tooth or **hurting** feet will show on your face.

> **Cherish a genuine good friend.** They are few and far between. Laugh with them, listen to them, learn from them, love them. That friend is a treasure beyond measure.

New **underwear** is a pleasure you can savor in secret. Whether it is cotton, satin, silk, or even a poly blend, it feels good. High cut, bikini cut, low cut, French cut or whatever (that means thong), it's fresh, unused and untried. I wish such a choice had been available when I was younger (back in the "old days"). I like the colors and some of the patterns. I might even try a leopard one and keep it my secret. (Sorry, Victoria.)

One of my "quick-easy-delicious" recipes

Tuna Salad
(Doug's Favorite)

- 1 Large (12 oz.) can or 2 small (6 oz.) cans Starkist tuna fish packed in water. White solid Albacore is best. Drain well.
- 1 Large Granny Smith apple (others are OK but tart, crisp ones are best.) Chop with peeling into large chunks (about the size of a big peanut)
- 4 or 5 regular size sweet pickles (or dill) chopped smaller than apple chunks.
- 2 heaping tablespoons mayonnaise, Hellmann's or Duke's.

Mix all together except Mayo. Add mayo and mix gently again. Add more mayo if necessary to please you. Serve stuffed in a tomato or just on lettuce or a sandwich. Feeds 6 generously, or more if they don't like it. If they like tuna, they will like this. It is refreshing.

P.S. I prefer sweet pickles, but use dill now because of diabetes in our family. Cut down on the mayo and cut calories.

Your **dog** will try very hard to understand what you want him to do; then try very hard to do it. Your cat will know exactly what you want him to do; then he will walk off—tail high—and do exactly whatever he wants to do, because he just doesn't give a cat's meow (or a rat's ass). Winston Churchill is quoted as saying, "Dogs look up to us. Cats look down on us. Hogs look upon us as equals."

Don't blame anything on **"fate."** We have the capacity to make decisions. Many of the things that happen to us are the result of our own decisions. However, sometimes things happen that we will never understand this side of eternity. "Now we see through a glass darkly . . . but then face to face." (I Corinthians 13) "Lean not to thy own understanding . . ."

Chocolate is my favorite comfort food.
I'd give it up, but I'm no quitter.
However, I vow to ration it daily.

Don't let your children (or you) pick at a scab that forms on skinned knees, cuts, bug bites, etc. The scab is **God's bandaid**. It protects and helps rebuild the skin cells. When the wound is well, the scab will fall off. This is not true for all wounds.

Never take any one else's prescription **medicines**—even if it is a family member or a friend. You may have similar symptoms, but it could affect you differently—even seriously.

Never, never give any of your children any medicines that were prescribed for another of your children without consulting with your doctor. The amount of dosage or strength may not be the same or it could interact differently.

Don't **despair**, time heals all wounds. It can take a long long time, even years; but if you try to help, it might happen sooner though it may leave a scar on your heart.

Be sure to teach your children at an early age to cover their mouths when **yawning**, not to talk with their mouths full, or chew gum in church.

The **farmers' market** is a wonderful place to go on an early summer's morning. You get first choice on all the fresh, home grown vegetables and fruits, plus the farmers (and their wives) are so interesting to you and you to them. They are really "down to earth." Have a conversation with them; they can size you up in a New York minute.

Don't just "let yourself go." Always try to look nice and fit the occasion as to dress and makeup. That means being clean and well groomed whether wearing jeans, a sweat shirt, or your Sunday-best. Clean hair, finger nails, teeth and body are a must. There is no reason to be sloppy or **smell bad**. Of course, there are exceptions—after a tough game, gardening or hunting and fishing, working on the car, after a hard workout at the gym, etc.—but with a bath and fresh clothes it can be said "you clean up good."

Being comfortable does not have to mean being sloppy.

Just because you do not want to believe something does not mean that it is not true. It could be; it probably is. Find out. Face it. If it is not true, be glad. If it is, **act**.

If you cannot find your favorite **kitchen knife**, look in the dishwasher.

Most women look better with good makeup and a good **hair style** and cut. Pale, washed out and droopy is not attractive. A touch of blush, a dab of lipstick can do wonders in just a few seconds.

Beans are good anytime, except perhaps breakfast (though your dad loved pork 'n beans in the Navy for breakfast with cornbread). There are green snap beans, bush beans, rattle snake beans, Kentucky wonders, string beans, shelly beans (big and plump that you shell), pole beans, purple beans (that turn green like magic while cooking and others that I do not know about. We love Kentucky wonders and purple beans best, but you have to string them before snapping. They are all good seasoned with fat—back, boiling meat, steak of lean, or bacon drippings and served with fresh tomatoes, green onions and cornbread. Cook as long as you want to . . . Yum!

Hate corrodes the vessel that carries it.

Purple hull **peas**, crowder and black eyed peas are all delicious. Also butter-beans, especially the small green ones. Buy them already shelled if possible. They cost more but are certainly worth it. Cook like you do the green beans and serve with the same side dishes. Yum! There is a small white pea called a "lady pea" that's a favorite but not easy to find and butter peas.

For best results creaming **butter** and sugar, allow butter to soften to room temperature (not melted) first.

At last! Help for **colicky** babies (and their parents) that makes sense and works. *The Happiest Baby on the Block,* written by pediatrician Harvey Karp gives a prescription for a quiet baby he calls "The Five S's." "Babies don't need freedom. They need the protection and security they felt inside the womb."

1. Swaddling
2. Side/stomach position
3. Shhing
4. Swinging
5. Sucking

❀ ✿ ❀

There is a remedy, hundreds and thousands of years old, for tension, irritability, nervousness, anger and worry. It eases and soothes and relaxes—guaranteed! Often it is free, but some are willing to pay a high price for it—their jobs, their families, their lives. The smallest dosage is called **"boudoir cheesecake"** and just a barely sweet taste is often effective. Men like it so much that they always want more (sooner or later). If your husband is suffering from any of those miserable symptoms, a dose of "boudoir cheesecake" is a tried and true prescription. The rest is up to you—two.

"Home Alone" is not a tough row to hoe for a wife and mother who is constantly busy with her family. Just a few hours (even 30 minutes) of peace and quiet are treasured moments and are much appreciated. My daughter Candy used to say, "Mama wants a piece of quiet."

If you are a **hostess**, it is your duty to be gracious, hospitable and to make your guests feel at home—even if you wish they were.

The 18th year is typically the time of greatest conflict *between parent and child*, but the 13th and 14th years are commonly the *most difficult 24 months in life for the youngster*. It is during this adolescent period that self doubt and feelings of inferiority reach an all time high (according to Dr. Dobson of *Focus on the Family*.) Perhaps this information will help you have a better **understanding** of your children.

Egg whites will keep in fridge for two days and in freezer for two months. They can be used for meringues, angel food cakes, soufflés or scrambled for folks who don't want the high cholesterol.

Please do not try to keep a large dog all day in a small apartment. It is almost cruel and inhuman treatment. If you really love that dog, find him a bigger **dog house**.

'Tis said that music is a **universal language,** and laughter has no foreign accent. Think about that!

Breakfast is the most important meal of the day! Your body has fasted all night. It is time to break-your-fast. Children who eat breakfast do better at school. Whatever job is done before noon is done better in any workplace if breakfast had been eaten. This has been proven in numerous scientific tests and studies. Be sure your child has food to eat before school—toast, eggs, meat, milk, cereal, bacon, fruit, (even pizza) to give them a head start on the day.

When the rain is pouring down, it's small comfort to realize you have two **umbrellas** in the car, which is parked four blocks from where you are.

Some days (when you have several children going in all directions, to school, ball practices, piano lessons, etc., etc., etc.) face the day by waking with a smile and saying, "Good morning. Let the **stress** begin." Try to make the smile last through the day.

Chocolate is a soul food. It helps relieve stress. Dark chocolate is best. (Don't overdose.)

Thousands of years ago cats were considered gods. They have not forgotten this. (Sign in pet store)

Being a **single parent** is the hardest job in the world, the challenge of a lifetime—for moms or dads. Earning a living, care of kids, homework, meals, ball games, cleaning, bills, insurance, banking, etc., plus finding times for loving hugs. Also finding energy to meet emotional and social needs. It's enough to exhaust the strongest person. The only answer to all these pressures is for the rest of us to give a helping hand and practical assistance. Single parents need to know that someone is willing to help share their burden. Find a way!! (In some cases, it may be best not to involve <u>your</u> husband.)

Try to **support** your home town merchants.

Efficiency experts divide workday hours into two basic categories: 1. Productive, and 2. After lunch (how 'bout a nap?)

Instead of sticking every **perennial** you find at the nursery in your garden (been there and done that), repeat groups of the same plants and echo the colors for a savvy vista. More of the same is better than a hodge-podge of random plantings. Group, group, group! No soldiers marching in a row, please.

Breakfast is the most important meal of the day.

> You will discover that the person who **talks** the most very often has the least to say.

Different colors that blend in your **flower garden** present a good show. For instance, blue, purple, pink, lavender, white and gray for cools; and red, yellow, hot pink and oranges for hots—you can always mix in white.

Boys **pee**. Girls tinkle or "answer the call of nature." Pee is a male word. 'Tis better for ladies to tinkle.

There's a very important four-letter word to remember when cooking: E-G-G-S . . . **S-L-O-W** (ly) and low heat.

When you marry, you become a bronco buster. There are lots of bumps and jerks and ups and downs (just hold on). Sometimes you may fall off—real down (get up and try again). Marriage is not a smooth ride, but can be exciting and wonderful. It is usually worth the journey. (Unless the horse turns out to be an ass!)

Riches and wealth can buy you anything you want except—health, happiness, and love.

Chocolate is good for you! Yes, it is combined with sugar and fat. That's why it tastes so good. It contains a high level of a chemical called pheno which has been shown to help decrease the risk of heart disease and lower LDL cholesterol—the bad kind. . . . Now get this—it also affects the levels of brain chemicals including the three which are called the chemical of love. They are the same substances that are released in response to romance. Eat it in moderation. It's worth the indulgence. Pass the double fudge brownies, please.

Your skin is like a **sponge**. It can soak in so much and then it is saturated. Lathering on more cream or oil is wasteful. Rub in a reasonable amount, not gobs. Some may be reapplied often, such as suntan oil, because the wind, water, and sun dry it up.

Growing up with **pets** actually lessens the likelihood of allergies (frogs, snakes, and spiders are not included). Children who have dogs and cats in the home have a significantly reduced risk of developing common allergies— some by 50 percent or more!

"That's the opposite of what we expected to find," said Dr. Dennis Ownby, chief of the Medical College of Georgia's Section of Allergy and Immunology and lead investigator on the study. In fact, children raised with two or more dogs or cats had 45 percent less hyper-reactivity. "It's very significant," Ownby said. "This contributes to the mounting evidence that the things allergists have believed for years and parents have lived by are wrong." (from a *Fit for Life* article by Steve Infanti)

❀ ✿ ❀

If **reading** gives you pleasure, you will never be alone.

❀ ✿ ❀

Other than making **lemonade**, there's lots of good uses for lemons! Clean copper pots. Juice often is used as an antidote for nausea (mix with a little water). Grinding peels in disposal keeps it smelling fresh, and putting peels around plants needing acidity helps fertilize. Lemons also add color and shape to a fruit arrangement or just a bowl of lemons is pleasing.

When dining in a nice restaurant, attending a wedding reception or other functions where part of the enjoyment is conversing with friends, family or other acquaintances, **background music** is quiet and lovely with the tempos and melodies changing while guests are almost unaware of the comfortable, agreeable feeling set by the music. That is the way it should be—background music.

Today it is difficult to have such a mood when attending any of the above mentioned occasions. There is no such thing as a pleasant or delightful conversation because people must shout at each other to be heard. By the time the evening is over, you're very likely to have a sore throat or headache. This is because the music is not in the background. It is blasted forth in a loud mélange of noise as if the band thinks the louder they play, the better they are. WRONG! Such "music" is more appropriate for teenage dances or other types of celebrations.

If you are a hostess, plan the music according to the festivity and audience they are playing for. You are paying for the entertainment, so check it out before the main event. Be sure the band understands that louder is not better. Turn down the volume so guests can hear and enjoy conversations.

Despair, grief and depression can harm you mentally, emotionally and physically. Help can come from sympathy, counseling or even drugs, but after all is said and done, you may still have sadness. That is something you have to take care of all on your own, and sad can last a long, long time. It can come and go; but, always comes back usually and fortunately in less and less degrees. Time heals. You can handle it.

> It is not necessary to dust everyday . . . mainly only when company is coming. The rest of the time let the dust protect your furniture.

Remember to have both the adult-strength medicine and the appropriate strength for children in your **medicine chest**. Don't try to just "cut down" adult medicine to fit your child. Age and weight are a factor. It's dangerous to guess! Throw away expired medication.

 Go easy! Easy! **Easy on perfume**. You don't want the scent to precede you into a room by five minutes or to overwhelm the people with you in the car or elevator. One friend I have sprays it in front of herself and then walks through it. Sounds like good "scents" to me.

Witches Brew

(alias "The Green")

"The green" is the answer I always get from your daddy, when I ask, "Which jell-o salad shall I make?" It will serve 8-10 people; and if any is left over, will keep in the fridge for a week. It only lasts for two days at our house.

- 1 small package of Lime jell-o.
- 1 small package of Lemon jell-o.
- $1^2/_3$ cups of boiling water

Stir together well and cool slightly.
Then with wire whisk, stir in:
- 1 cup mayo
- 1 small can condensed milk.

Next add:
- 1 (12-16 oz.) carton small curd cottage cheese
- $15^1/_2$ oz. can crushed pineapple with juice
- 1 cup chopped pecans.

Pour into big flat casserole (can be cut into blocks) or large (6-8 cup) mold or 2 smaller molds. Lightly spray mold with Pam. Let set in fridge for 2 or more hours. Looks pretty garnished with mandarin oranges, Kiwi, grapes or strawberries.

My friends call it "witches brew" because it looks a bit yucky with the pineapple, cheese lumps, and pecans floating in the green stuff.

"Oh, innocent victims of cupid,

Remember this terse little verse;
>   To let a fool kiss you is stupid,
>   To let a kiss fool you is worse."

— Unknown

> Where you've been is done and gone. It's **where you're going** and how you get there that's important. Keep on keeping on.

Success is not an entitlement; it has to be earned. Start from scratch and keep scratching.

Call your **mother**! Occasionally is good, more often is better.

Old Indian saying: "To understand a man, **walk** in his moccasins." Do this and your party will be a success; a business will have more satisfied customers; a teacher will better understand her pupils, and you will be a better mother and wife—if you'll just try to put yourself in their place, see what they see, feel what they feel.

Cooking eggs eggsactly right:

Preheating skillet over medium heat before adding eggs keeps them from sticking (put about a teaspoon of oil or butter skillet first). To make fluffier scrambled eggs use water or milk—3 teaspoons per egg—add salt, and beat with a fork or whisk until combined. Do not overheat when cooking—use heavy non-stick pan or well seasoned skillet. Do not use a pan too big or eggs will spread out and cook too quickly. There's an ongoing argument over whether to use milk or water for the fluffiest eggs. I vote for water.

Slow cooking (crock pot): Browning your meat

and sautéing the vegetables before putting in pot is not necessary BUT it adds flavor and color to the finished dish. Do not add cooked pasta or rice until the last 30 minutes of cooking period, else they will be gummy. Bell peppers, hot peppers, and cayenne get bitter in a slow cooker, but can be added the last 30 minutes. Cut carrots, turnips, and potatoes into thin pieces because they take longer to cook than meats. If adding liquid, use undiluted canned broths or stock.

When in doubt, add more **wine**—to the pot and your glass. (Sage wisdom to cooks and connoisseurs.)

A sweet, loving **daughter** is a joy and blessing for a life-time, and the Lord gave me four. "My cup runneth over."

No matter how many pounds I gain or lose, my right foot still weighs 70 miles an hour.

The **older** you get, the quicker Christmas comes.

"I think I've finally **"grown-up,"** because I now can eat brownies and salads with nuts." Someone remarked to me today. Truthfully, everyone doesn't like nuts mixed into their food—especially children and men—keep them in a bowl or bag, please. However, age, tasting, and trying can eventually win them over except the ones who will pick out the nuts the rest of their life. That remark today was made by my 45-year-old sophisticated daughter.

Life is **simpler** if you remember the things you ought not to forget and forget the things you ought not remember. Easier said than done.

You must act **enthusiastic** to be enthusiastic.

"Church shoes" are very nice looking but usually too tight, too short, and must be kicked off immediately after church (maybe even in the car).

It is difficult to be creative, excited or have a good attitude when you're not feeling **up to par**.

You can forget God, but He never forgets you. (Thank God.)

They say **"wine is good for you,"** white, red or (?) pink. I've never cared for it except in the last eight years or so. I like to be "in the pink" usually inexpensive, but tastes good, too. They say "Wine improves with age." I guess it's true, because the older I get the better I like it. Madam Pompadour once declared, "Champagne is the only wine that leaves a woman beautiful after drinking it."

Don't equate or rate **human worth** with flawless beauty or handsomeness. It cannot be lasting. An old and true saying is, "Don't judge a book by its cover."

"**Absence** makes the heart grow fonder" is an old saying, but I think we might add that according to the length of absence "May make the heart start to wander." A similar word with a totally different but important meaning is "abstinence." I think perhaps most of us need to practice it occasionally—with alcohol, candy, cigarettes, sex, fatty foods, too much togetherness. (You name it.)

Don't let yourself get hooked on **laxatives**. Eat bran (flakes, muffins, etc.) for breakfast, prunes or prune juice, if necessary. Drink lots of water and exercise. You will find things moving smoothly after a few days. Stress can be a bowel-blocker. Don't strain; hemorrhoids can be a terrible SITuation.

> The cheapest **face lift** is a smile.

Gossip is usually interesting even if it is about people you don't know, but don't pass it on. It could be true or not.

Genuine **laughter** is truly the best medicine—replenishes your mind, picks up your spirit and actually makes you feel better. Just a smile improves your outlook to others and yourself.

Dear One: You may think that now Momma has had her say, but not so. When I am dead and gone (in the far distant future, I hope), you will still hear me **voice my opinion** now and then. Sometime I hear your precious grandmother in my head. Sometimes I can even see her if I close my eyes. Someday this will happen to your children, too. You are their mama and you will still have your say.

Don't open your mouth unless you can improve the silence.

Chocolate is good for what ails you. It's a dark, luxurious, rich experience. It's dreamy and creamy, lovey dovey—erotic, exotic—delicious, nutritious—magic and witchy (a little bitchy)—silky and milky—divine and dark, sublime and stark—invigorates, rejuvenates—a pleasure giver, like cupid's quiver—spirit lifter, perfect GIFTer—a healing balm and soothing calm—a tasty storm, a comfort warm. It's also stimulating and quite pleasantly addictive. 'Tis said that Casanova swore by chocolate, so forget Viagra and think of chocolate, the magic potion.

One of my divorced lady friends defined **ALIMONY** as bounty on the mutiny.

Communication is a type of medicine. Talk, talk, talk, to a friend who listens sympathetically (or not) about your love life, or lack thereof, about grief and sorrow, about unfairness, your health, worries, children, mistakes, ideas, family problems, etc. A good listener is good medicine, but must have one special ingredient not found at the pharmacy— the ability to keep her mouth shut about your affairs! You always feel better if you can share your problems and joys with a good listener. It is more useful if she does not offer advice unless asked for (not that you have to take it).

Attitude is everything.

 We all need to get close to **nature**— a garden, a forest, birds, animals, a sunrise or sunset, a river, a leaf, a nut. Examine and study (and wonder) how wondrously they are made. Even though we do not understand, we know they are not made by accident. 'Tis a marvelous plan. Take note: sitting next to a plastic fern does not count.

You can be lonely in a movie or at a parade with hundreds of people around you. **Lonely** does not just mean you are alone. It is an inside your head and heart thing. (Call your momma???)

Best Baked Beans

(feeds a crowd 20-30)

- 1 Pound ground chuck
- 1 large onion, chopped
- 3 or 4 (31 oz.) cans pork and beans
- 2 to 4 tablespoons prepared mustard
- 2 to 4 tablespoons Worcestershire sauce
- ½ cup brown sugar
- ½ cup tomato catsup

Brown beef and pour off most of fat. Add chopped onions to beef as it browns. Put all ingredients in bean pot or big, deep casserole dish with lid. Cook in oven on low heat at 250 degrees for at least an hour. My friend cooks it sometime 3 or 4 hours at 250 degrees.

p.s. You can adjust this recipe to your taste and time, and it still is good! Perhaps that's its charm.

Modesty and restraint are two traits that ladies should employ; but there is a time and place for everything. You must decide where and when these qualities can possibly be a bit diluted (or exempt, if ever).

> ## Are you **thick** and tired? Diet!

No matter how old we live to be, the Lord wants us to **bear fruit**. I have enjoyed five wonderful children, a comfortable home, a lovely marriage, three businesses to supply our finances, 11 grandchildren, dear friends and good health. I have borne and been thankful for all this fruit of life. (Count your blessings, name them one by one.) Along the way there have been bumps in the road of the fruit truck—the death of a child, cancer, financial difficulties; but we have not been promised a rose garden. Every one has problems. Usually we would not trade ours for theirs. "They shall bring forth fruit in old age; they shall be fat and flourishing." (Psalm 92:14) I hope this book counts as good fruit. I appreciate "approval" of fat and am still looking forward to flourishing.

When you are young, you think that **time** moves slowly. It seems that forever is far away. But in truth, time moves quickly, and the older you get it speeds up! Tempus fugit.

Learn to identify **snakes**. Some of the crawling ones are not dangerous. All of the ones with two legs are (male and female).

❀ ✿ ❀

Shakespeare's recipe for a snake-in-the grass: "Look like the innocent flower, but be the serpent under't."

(from Macbeth)

❀ ✿ ❀

Cheery, waving-wildly **forsythia**—how welcome are the yellow flowers dancing willy-nilly in the breezes every year! Just plant them in a sunny spot (three or more together) for one of spring's loosely choreographed ballets. Please do not stop the dance by pruning them into spiky balls!!! Branches will bloom after being cut and put in water inside. Cuttings four to six inches long usually will root with no problems just by sticking them into the wet ground.

❀ ✿ ❀

Cut out the **mayo!** One tablespoon of mayonnaise has 100 calories, 99% from fat. A tablespoon of mustard has about 15 calories and one gram of fat. Just cutting out mayo from your diet could help you lose 10-15 pounds in a year. "Hold the mayo! It's a no no."

When you are **afraid**, read Isaiah 41:10 "Fear not for I am with you: be not dismayed" . . . and John 14:27 "Peace I leave with you . . . Let not your heart be troubled, neither be afraid."

Attitudes change with learning.

It is better to **hire yourself out** to work which is beneath you rather than become dependent on others. Better in mind, body and spirit. You will not be obligated and will be accomplishing something.

> The **winning recipe:** high in fiber, low in saturated fat, is sugar-free and low in cholesterol, has no salt and no preservatives—and tastes good! If you have it, please send me a copy.

"Nothing in **excess**" is a good rule—too much food, exercise, work, play, drinking (sometime even companionship) can cause problems. Somewhere in there, some way you need to find a balance that is best for body, mind and spirit. However, I am not sure an excess of money would be bad. If I ever find out, I will let you know; but darlings, don't hold your breath (unless it starts growing on trees).

Spotted this on a cute tee shirt—

Here's to good women:
May we know them. (I do)
May we be them. (I try)
May we raise them. (I have)

Make a **list** of what you need to accomplish for a week. It's a good feeling when you can check each job "done," and then you get to eat a chocolate double-dip ice cream cone or take a nap.

A new study shows that not getting enough **potassium** can raise your risk of stroke by 50%! Eat bananas, avocados, raisins, spinach, tomato juice, watermelon, orange juice and baked sweet potatoes.

It takes a long time to grow an old friend.
Recognize, cherish and treasure that person.
We are not allowed very many.

Cravings a no-no? Sometimes the faster you give in and have a portion of the food you are dying for, the better off you are. The trick is to have just a small serving and get it over with.

Personally I am not "hung up" on **laxatives**, but some of my friends are. Dr. Peter Gott in one of his columns states that chronic constipation commonly affects most of us as we age. He recommends 8 ounces of hot prune juice every morning or two or three table spoons of triple mix (equal portions of prune juice, bran, and applesauce) daily with extra fluids—"will do the trick." (His words not mine.)

Be generous with your compliments. Some of us can live two months on a good one.

Prayer can be good medicine. "We are not out to prove that a deity exists," says professor Dianne Becker of Johns Hopkins, recipient of two NIH grants for research on prayer. "We are trying to see whether prayer has meaning to people that translates into biology, and affects a disease process."

"Medical acceptance has grown along with solid scientific data on prayers impact," says Dr. Dale Mathews of Georgetown University. He estimates that 75 percent of studies on spirituality have confirmed health benefits. "If prayer were available in **pill form**, no pharmacy could stock enough of it."

As you well know, **Winston Churchill** has long been admired by your daddy. He has read most of his books (some more than once) and loves to quote the tongue in cheek, usually humorous and terse remarks. Recently he read an amusing one from a George Will column as follows: "Churchill tells about a man who received a message from a friend that his mother-in-law had died, asking for instructions. The reply was, 'Embalm! Cremate. Bury at sea . . . Take no chances!'"

If two **meetings** of equal importance are held at the same time, and the same people should be in attendance, and one meeting offers snacks or a meal, the meeting with food will have better numbers, even if they have to pay to eat.

> When in line at the check-out register with a cart full of **groceries,** take note if the person behind you has just a few items. Invite them to go ahead of you. They will be happy; you will feel good; and maybe someone will do you the same favor some day.

My dears, you have to accept that some days, you are the **pigeon**—and some days you are the statue (not a pretty sight). Keep an umbrella handy when the "shit" hits the fan. (Sorry, but that four-letter word is the only one to fit this situation). Learn to duck.

A **good hostess** won't neglect the non-drinkers at a brunch or party. For a brunch other than bloody marys and mimosas, offer unusual bottled juices, like pear and mango, plus tomato (some spicy) and fresh citrus juices. For afternoon parties, add crystal pitchers of daiquiris, margaritas or sangria, garnished with fruit slices or wedges. All these are also delicious at night, but you will probably have to add individual cocktails.

A hot love is the only fire against which there is no insurance.

A devastating four-letter word is **FEAR**. Former President Roosevelt said, "The only thing we have to fear is fear itself." We are afraid of what people will say, afraid of getting out of our comfort zone, afraid of being laughed at, afraid of failure, etc., etc., etc. A turtle never gets anywhere until he sticks his neck out. Fear is a devastating emotion that does more harm than good. You can overcome it. The Lord is on your side. Remember that!!!!

Just because a food is **fat-free** does not mean it is calorie-free. Many foods have the same amount of calories as the original version. Check the facts on the food label.

Even writers on spirituality concede that science may never prove that prayer can heal others, but adds Dr. Machell Crucoff of Duke University, "That doesn't mean that people shouldn't take advantage of this wonderful tool right at their fingertips." Dr. Koeing, also of Duke University, states that prayer, "Whether for oneself or others affects the quality, if not the quantity of life. It boosts the morale, lowers agitation, loneliness, and enhances the ability to **cope** in men, women, the elderly, the young, the healthy and the fit." Believe it or not, but . . . WHY NOT?

> **It is wise to settle an argument by being fair and giving a choice: They can agree with you or be wrong.**

Freezing cooked chicken in broth keeps up to six months, without broth about a month.

A beloved retired minister returned to our church recently to fill the pulpit of our regular preacher who was absent that Sunday. His sermon was about Peter, whom Jesus loved very much, and you know what Peter did!! (Read Mark 14:29-30, and 66-72). One statement the minister made has stuck in my head and heart. He said, "Perfection is not a requisite for **discipleship**." Aren't we glad? Thank God!!

Breaking-up is hard to do—and yet it could save breaking your spirit or mind or body (or all three) on down the road. Think about it.

> Good **habits** are hard to keep and easy to break. Bad habits are easy to keep and hard to break. It takes time to acquire a good habit. It just takes a minute to break it. When a good habit becomes spontaneous, you've got it made. It's a practice that will add pleasure to your life.

Refresh and repair your body (including your skin) the easy way—rest and sleep. Most biological activities that repair and restore your body take place while you are at rest—sleeping especially. What a comfortable way to heal thyself. That's why doctors prescribe bed rest.

Dry **rough feet**, especially heels, will improve if you rub them with a hydrating foot cream or lotion; then pull on loose, light-colored cotton socks for the night. If you just cannot sleep in socks, <u>cut the toes</u> out and let your feet breathe. It works.

A good decorator is **worth** the money.

Hair spray and eye glasses are a bad combination. Before spraying remove your glasses far away from the area. It is difficult to see with spray on your glasses, and also difficult to clean it off.

❀ ✿ ❀

❀ ✿ ❀

Christians see the crucifixion as a victory instead of a defeat because of the **resurrection**. Jesus walked, talked, cooked breakfast and showed his wounds to his apostles after He died. Hundreds of people saw him, many wrote about seeing and being with him and told what He said. Nowhere is there a sustained claim that the resurrection did not happen.

❀ ✿ ❀

"Believe on me and you shall have eternal life—this day you shall be with me in Paradise" (no call waiting—to the thief on the cross who believed). "I go to prepare a place for you" (RSVP not necessary). "In my father's house there are many mansions." (There is plenty of room for you and me.)

❀ ✿ ❀

Every day we beat our own previous record for number of days we have **stayed alive**.

Sometimes we get **"a hankering for"** special food we haven't eaten in a while, or people and places we haven't seen in a long time. In the south, we might hanker for turnip greens, cornbread, catfish, peach cobbler, boiled custard, or fried fruit pies—yum yum. After a spell away from my children and grandchildren, I get a hankering to see them. Once in a while I want to visit the old home place, my high school or college, the drug store where we used to "hang out." Certain smells, pictures, or conversations can instigate "a hankering for." Hankering is really not just a southern thing, but it is a descriptive southern expression.

The **worst abuse** in the world is child abuse, and it is world wide. The *Memphis Commercial Appeal*, reports that child abuse and neglect rose in 2001 for the second straight year, the last year for which data is available. There is no telling what the numbers are in other countries, many in which no one counts because children don't count, especially girls. The article states that about 1,300 died in 2001 from abuse or neglect (that is just the ones known about). Children who are too small, too weak, too innocent, need to be protected, not neglected. We cannot save nor change the world, but we can "brighten the corner where we are." Teach your children to help those who are not able to help themselves. Do what you can, when you can, wherever you can. A child is the world's future.

The **illusion of control** is the next best stress relief to actual control (in the work place). The third most common headache is work place stress. Have you ever changed the temperature on your office thermostat only to have nothing happen? If so, the following news will not surprise you. According to engineers, most office thermostats are not attached to anything: They exist to give us the illusion of control. Speaking of illusions, the "closed door button" on most elevators is also non functioning, unless you have a special key to activate it. This is from a column called "Working Wounded," by Bob Rosner in the *Austin American Statesman*.

Mama said, "If the **illusion of control** doesn't work, use an old remedy. Take three deep breaths. Take two aspirins. Drink a large glass of water and look forward to quitting time."

Along with the idea that some foods need to rest: a friend told me her mother once had a cook who explained why soups, spaghetti, and some other foods are better after a day or night in the refrigerator. "It needs to set there and get to **know itself**." No one could say it better.

There are times when we all need an attitude adjustment.

"A **woman's place** is in the home" (old adage)
". . . after she gets off from work." (new addition to old adage). Being a stay-at-home mom is a personal choice. I do believe it is important for mothers with young children to be at home with them as much as possible; but often due to family circumstances, it is not always possible. There is no doubt that the person you hire to care for your children cannot give them a mother's love and care. Staying home is not an easy job. Actually the term "stay-at-home mom" is out of vogue because stay-at-home moms are on the go. Most of them are usually in the car transporting their children to ball practice, music lessons, gym, birthday parties, and school or picking them up from the previously mentioned places and trying to work in dental and doctor appointments, grocery shopping, dropping or picking up clothes at the cleaners, attending school meetings, games, and programs, etc., etc., etc. Somewhere in there, mom plans, prepares and serves meals. Those who demean mom for being homemakers and staying at home need to travel in their footsteps (car) just one day. It's exhausting and often stressful. You'll agree her job is not "just a piece of cake." Those who try to balance all of this with a career or other jobs, need all the help (and sometimes sympathy) they can get from husbands and family members. Blessings on loving, caring, trying mothers wherever you are. (Mother's day 5-11-03)

Savory Oyster Crackers
(old friend's recipe)

- 16 oz. box or package of oyster crackers
- 1 cup of vegetable oil
- 1 package original Hidden Valley Ranch dressing (dry)
- $\frac{1}{2}$ teaspoon garlic salt
- $\frac{1}{2}$ teaspoon dill weed
- $\frac{1}{2}$ teaspoon lemon pepper

Empty all dry ingredients into large bowl. Stir gently. Add oil and stir occasionally until oil is absorbed (several times within two hours). Store in canister to keep crisp and dry. Can use cookie or cake tins. Serve with soup, salad, or just as a tasty snack.

P.S. She said they are so good you should double the recipe. She was right!

Note: 'Twas a brave man who first an oyster ate.

Know the difference: Plant *annuals* for lots of color and bloom for one season. They are cheap for the amount of pleasure they quickly give—many from springtime all through the summer if planted in their favorite places—some shade, some hot sun.

Perennials bloom for more than one year, sometimes for several years or even generations. Of course this depends on planting them in their favored sites plus proper preparation of beds. Quoting from one of my not-green-thumb neighbors, "A perennial is a plant that comes back from its roots every year—if it had lived."

> Every life has its dark and fearful hours. **Happiness** comes from choosing which to remember.

The **best gardening advice** I can give you is don't do as I do. What knowledge about gardening I have comes from magazines, newspapers, books and friends—not actual successes. (As anyone can see when they drive past our house.) There are a few pretty spots—mostly lavishly planted pots that put on a big show with little care. My "will do" can't seem to keep up with my "want to." However, I am very thankful for the perennial friends in my garden of life who bloom year 'round and never fail me.

If your husband leaves the house in a **huff** after an argument (whether you win or lose), get the last word by saying something nice, sweet, or loving (or all three) as he goes out the door. It will make him "off balance" for the rest of the day—and he may come home in a better mood.

Don't be discouraged by a mistake. Some of the best ideas in the world have been the result of a mistake.

Strokes: To soothe the "savage beast," stroking often works wonders. Stroke or gently rub his hand or arm or neck and shoulders—on down his back or other places (feet, maybe?) This almost always calms the stormy waters and soothes away stress. Cats purr, dogs wag their tails, and people relax and emit sighs of delight. This works on the opposite sex (us) too, Nothing beats the personal-touch-effect (except winning the lottery).

Don't make **hamburgers cry**. That's what happens when you keep mashing them with the spatula. You are squeezing out the juicy tears. They do cook quicker, but you are toughening up the meat. It's like cardboard and just as tasty. Use the spatula only for turning—out a fat juicy hamburger.

145

Icing is quick and easy with just 2 ingredients. Combine one 3.75 ounce package instant pudding mix (any flavor) with 2 cups whipping cream, not whipped. Keep the 2 layer frosted cake in the fridge until serving time.

Three wise men:

"Be kind for every one you meet is fighting a hard battle."
Plato

"We make a living by what we get; we make a life by what we give." *Winston Churchill.*

"Remember happiness doesn't depend on who you are or what you have; it depends on what you think."
Dale Carnegie

Three wise women

would have asked directions, arrived on time, helped deliver the baby, cleaned the stables, made a casserole, brought practical gifts and there would be peace on earth. (Author unknown—a woman for sure and certain).

You marry for **better or worse.** If the worse gets unbearable for your family, and you have tried everything and used all the help you could find, you may ask yourself, "Are we better off with him or without him?" Then act accordingly.

Fun and games will add much pleasure to your lifestyle both early and late. Try to participate in playing a sport—volleyball, tennis, golf, softball, basketball, even shuffleboard. Chess, board games, tennis and golf can be enjoyed to a ripe old age and are good for your brain and body. If you cannot play or are not athletically inclined, be a spectator. Taking part one way or another is good for you both mentally and physically plus broadening your friendships and improving your personality. Yea Team!!!!!

> Brown **eggs** are not healthier than white eggs.
> The breed of the hen determines the color of the eggs.

Danger: End Zone. This is the last item, I promise, about plumbing problems. They are so stressful (and can be caused by stress) and uncomfortable and concern so many people who suffer a food "roadblock" on the way to its proper destination. This is called constipation. There is not a detour. Eat right, exercise, drink lots of water and see a doctor if the problem does not improve. Don't strain! That leads to worse problems called hemorrhoids which are painful and often require surgery—not a pretty site. Take care of your problem before it builds roadblocks, and flush your problems away.

Your husband must **"face the music"** even if he does-n't like the tune. Life does not often play his favorite song. There is always someone taller, bigger, or stronger than he is. There is always someone with a better job, who drives a newer car, makes more money and seems to get all the breaks. A man's world is a dog-eat-dog rat race. Every day he takes his place at the starting gate and chugs along 'til the day's finish line doing the best he can for you, for his family, for his own hopes and dreams. Help him dance to the music with rhythm and verve.

❀ ✿ ❀

One sincere compliment from a lady is worth 10 compliments from a man and is much harder to merit.

❀ ✿ ❀

Toothpicks are used in elegant surroundings, with beau-tiful, tasty appetizers or dips for example. They are also used in a most unsightly manner by those who know no better than to chew on one and pick their teeth in public. Actually though, this little exposé is in praise of the toothpick for cleaning purposes . . . only in private, of course. Nothing can beat it including brushing or flossing or both. If you doubt, brush your teeth as usual; then floss. Now use a toothpick to clean teeth. Aha! There's more tidbits and tar-tar lurking there . . . so keep some toothpicks handy in your bathroom, a very cheap help for healthy teeth and gums.

Good advice about the **birds and bees.** A friend told me that she remarked to her husband it seemed time their young teen age boys were told about sex. "OK" he said. "You tell them." "Oh no," she replied. "You're a doctor. You should explain it to them."—and so he took them into the bedroom, closed the door and said, "Keep your pants zipped unless you have to pee." Much later, she just happened innocently to mention that his explanation did not seem to take long. "Oh," he grinned, "they already knew." On reflection she thinks he realized she was listening just outside the door.

> **"Faith** sees the invisible, believes the unbelievable, and receives the impossible." —*Corrie Ten Boom*

If you buy any item from a store, take it home, and it is not satisfactory (lamp too tall, clothes don't fit, etc., etc.)— **return items** to store as soon as possible. They cannot sell it if it is not in their store. Also, be sure you get credit for return or money back with your receipt.

Cold water helps some **injuries**, insect stings, sprains, burns all feel better, at least temporarily.

"One woman is fair, another is wise, another virtuous, but 'til all graces be in one woman, one woman shall not come in my graces." (From Shakespeare's *Much Ado About Nothing*). Ladies, it has been ever thus. Men do not realize nor admit that they are not **perfect,** but expect us to be. Sometimes we convince them we are. Sometimes they find out we aren't, but we knew all the time they are not. Still, men are a wonderful pastime—sometimes for the rest of your life.

A bar of unwrapped fresh-smelling soap in your lingerie drawer makes a delightful **sachet,** and is long lasting.

'Tis one of life's greatest **paradoxes,** that "when we are born and come into the world, we cry while those around us smile; but if we live our lives as God intended—when we die, we can smile while those around us cry." (This is a remark by the late evangelist Angel Martinez quoted by Jim Davidson.)

It would be wise for your children to learn to speak Spanish, French and Chinese. Of course, they need to speak correct English first. The more **languages** they know, the better. The world is getting smaller every day. Good communications is the key to understanding.

Easy Pots de Crème
(A winner, can be made a day ahead.)

- 1 (16 oz.) pack semi sweet chocolate morsels
- 2 tablespoons of sugar
- pinch of salt
- 1 egg
- 1 teaspoon vanilla
- 1 teaspoon instant coffee
- $3/4$ cups scalded milk
- $1/2$ pint heavy cream, whipped
- 1 oz. unsweetened chocolate, grated for garnish

Put first 6 ingredients in blender; heat milk to boiling; pour into blender, cover; blend 1 minute. Pour into sherbet glasses or cups; chill several hours. Top generously with whipped cream and chocolate shavings. Serves four.

P.S. Don't worry about fat, sugar or calories. These are small servings! Not too much—not too little—just right for a delicious and impressive, elegant end to your meal.

(From a friend in Jackson, Mississippi)

OK! OK! I was **wrong, wrong, wrong**. I recant my comment about silk flowers, artificial flowers and fruit, even plastic flowers. Recently as a guest of my daughter at a lovely condo in Florida, I sat on a huge sofa in a huge living room looking at four huge, tall artificial plants and two small ones plus two more in the kitchen. There were also two in each bedroom, and one in each bathroom. I tried to visualize the rooms without them. They would have been stark and lifeless. Yes, the lifeless plants seem to give "life" to the room. Even man-made plants are better than no plants in some cases (restaurants, for one)—but please keep them shaped naturally and clean, not stiff and dusty. Still, God-made live plants are the most beautiful and desirable if they can be cared for.

This apology is especially for the florists and decorators who were outraged by my previous comments, several pages ago. Please accept it graciously,and do not ask for a refund on this book. (We cherish every purchase.)

After your husband has left for work and your children are gone to school, now that is one of the **best times** of the day. You can flop in your chair at the table, drink a cup of coffee and scan the newspaper. Then, fill and start the dishwasher and washing machine while you wonder what to fix for supper. However, if you still have little ones at home, you must omit those first two sentences.

Old Rhymes

(This one is very ,very old. Author unknown, but contributed by a friend <u>older</u> than I)

Men are queer creatures
Who stride about
They reach in their pockets
And pull things out.

They look important
And rock on their toes.
They pull the buttons
Off of their clothes.
(when they think you're
not looking,
they pick their nose.)

They'll give you a grin
And wink their eye.
They can make you laugh,
And make you cry.
Men are queer creatures
    But
I like men, don't you?

(this one is old)

My Momma told me if be goodie,
That she would buy me a rubber dollie.
So don't you tell her I've got a feller,
Or she won't buy me a rubber dollie.

A **brother** can be a blessing. He can offer comfort and support, be a "sounding-board"; and if he is a fun person with wit and humor, you are a lucky sister. (Aren't you!)

> It's not what **you say**, but the <u>way</u> you say it. (Think on that!)

Think **orchids** are too expensive? Wrong! They **give** you <u>more</u> bang for your buck. Buy orchids for house décor plants. They come in all sizes and colors—each a work of art. Think they're too difficult to care for? Wrong! The rising popularity of an orchid is its <u>resilience</u>. Your average potted house plant lasts about two weeks, longer, perhaps, but not as pretty or healthy. An orchid will last 3 to 4 months with almost no light and no water. It takes ten times more abuse. They are beautiful and make your room more elegant and serene. You deserve orchids (even though you still remember your date gave you a carnation corsage at the senior prom.)

In the daytime, before taking your seat in a restaurant, try to sit with your back to windows that may cause a **glare** if you face them.

When being seated in **nice restaurant**, try not to be placed by the kitchen doors or close to the restrooms or a service station where waiters keep ketchup, pitchers of water, etc. There will be people coming and going constantly by that table. If the hostess heads that way politely request another table before you are seated.

It is nice to **thank the waiter** who refills your water glass or coffee cup or performs any extra service (brings more butter or salad dressing, replaces fork you dropped on floor, etc., etc., etc.)

Memories may fade away, but a **heart-ache** never forgets.

If you feel like crying for no reason at all, or cry for any reason at all, you are probably **pregnant.** It is definitely best to be married at this time.

❀ ✿ ❀

Cherish your yesterdays; dream your tomorrows; but live your **todays**.

I think I'll just "pass on."

Sometimes people will say, "I am sorry
you lost your father." Others may say,
"I'm sorry your sister passed away."
All of these people are well meaning
and comforting; but if you don't mind,
I'd rather just "pass on." I've known for a long time where I
am going at the end of this life, and so—I'll just pass on to a
far better place, but hope I have times to whisper "Bye, dear
ones. See you later."

"Finally, brethren, whatsoever things are true,
whatsoever things are honest,
whatsoever things are just,
whatsoever things are pure,
whatsoever things are lovely,
whatsoever things are of good report;
if there be any virtue, and if there be any praise,
THINK ON THESE THINGS."

(Phillipians 4:8)

Last Words

Mama says...

This book is written now because my daughters have said, "Mama, you need to get the book you've been writing for 30 years published NOW because you need not think we are going to try to put all this stuff together after you're gone!" (They are such darling daughters.)

So there you have it . . . but I surely do not claim that it's all original. Many of these ideas are from my mother, grand-mother, aunt, and mother-in law. You have probably heard some of this from your mother. (We mothers are notorious for giving advice, often heard but not always followed!) Also, some of these thoughts are from books and newspapers.

If you are giving this book as a gift, here is a good suggestion to make it more personal plus adding a bit of your own charm; thumb through the book adding in the margins "Amen" or "How True" or another remark to anything that may correspond to something in your experience. There are some blank pages (so you don't have to use scraps like I did) in the back of the book just waiting for you to add some of your own advice, thoughts or ideas.

Let me hear from you,

Martha
P. O. Box 905
Corinth, MS 38834
cokeman@nadata.net

Profile

Martha Hammond, a native Mississippian, spent her early years in Corinth, Mississippi where she graduated from Corinth High School. Then she attended Ward Belmont College, a two-year finishing school for young ladies in Nashville, Tennessee. After graduation in 1950, she attended the University of Mississippi for one year, married Doug Hammond in 1951, and graduated from Belhaven College in Jackson, Mississippi.

Her husband was stationed in Norfolk, Virginia, with the U.S. Navy, so Martha spent the next four years in that area. Candy, her first child, was born in Norfolk in 1954. The family returned to Corinth in 1955 and has stayed there until this time, where she has been very active in civic, church, and volunteer activities. She also helped her husband in their three retail clothing and gift stores.

Martha is the mother of four girls; Candy, who died of leukemia when she was 10 years old; Shannon Umstattd of Austin, Texas; Courtney Love of Jackson, Mississippi; and Shelby Flaten of Dallas, Texas. She has one son, Barnett Douglas, Jr. who also resides in Dallas. Martha has 11 grand-children. She and Doug still live in Corinth, where they lead an active life in all aspects of their community.

This is your chance to "have your say."
(Fill in the blanks)

_____

_____

_____

_____

_____

_____

_____

_____

_____

_____

_____

_____

_____

_____

_____

_____

_____

_____

_____

_____

_____

_____

_____

_____

_____

_____

_____

_____

_____

This is your chance to "have your say."
(Fill in the blanks)

_____
_____
_____
_____
_____
_____
_____
_____
_____
_____
_____
_____
_____
_____
_____
_____
_____
_____
_____
_____
_____
_____
_____
_____
_____
_____
_____
_____
_____
_____
_____
_____
_____